WITH RHYME FOR REASON

CLARENCE R. THOMPSON

ISBN: 0615465552
ISBN-13: 9780615465555
Library of Congress Control Number: 2011904672
Thompson Photos, Prose and Poems

CONTENTS

INTRODUCTION

I did not set out to write a book of poems; instead the book evolved by chance. Perhaps I should explain. Some people doodle while engaged in deep thought about important issues. For some inexplicable reason, I dabble in rhyme. My poems, however, usually suffered the same fate—they were tossed in the trash can. One day my wife resurrected one from the trash. Somber discussion ensued and I decided to put them in a book.

Retirement has given me ample time to reflect on the issues that define my generation. I believe we've been careless in safeguarding our democracy, protecting the environment, addressing the health care crisis, and solving global problems. Our view of the issues is often based on one, or more, of these factors: financial self-interest, political persuasion, and religious ideology.

Likewise, we approach global matters based on national interest with little regard for how our decisions impact other nations. For instance the United States is the world's largest consumer of energy, yet we refuse to reduce carbon emissions for fear of adversely affecting Wall Street profits.

When faced with real or perceived threats, we sometimes resort to military solutions without engaging in thoughtful diplomacy, determining military objectives, forming alliances, planning an exit strategy, or considering the post-combat consequences. Military action is also dubiously combined with nation building in an attempt to force democracy on people from different backgrounds, cultures, and religions.

We intervene in the affairs of others while failing to put our own in order. Our quest for cheap labor to maximize profits has left our country too dependent on goods manufactured offshore. This trend contributes to unemployment and produces tremendous trade deficits. In addition we spend more on health care than most developed countries, but we rank low in health care outcomes. The unbridled greed of corporations and financial institutions has all but collapsed the American economy and contributed to a global recession. Political gridlock hinders our ability to find solutions to our problems and threatens future generations.

Feeling powerless to bring about significant change, I do what I can by reducing my carbon footprint, increasing my involvement in the political process, discussing issues with friends and family, and writing in verse. Along the way I've come to recognize the need for greater emphasis on intangibles such as love, hope, charity, and faith. They are far more important than net worth and have greater influence on the family, the neighborhood, and perhaps the global community.

The poems contained herein fall into eight broad categories. Each category is preceded by a short essay that provides context for the poems. I hope the combination of prose and verse will provoke thoughtful discussion and spawn a united effort to solve the challenges that face our nation. We must be informed, frank, and civil. There is no room for fear or gridlock—our challenges are too great. Competent leadership, an effective Congress, and a knowledgeable electorate are necessary to resolve these problems so we do not pass them on to our heirs. All the while we should focus on the intangibles and remember that it is in *God* we trust.

LOVE

Some people spend an entire lifetime seeking love. They search for it in the workplace, at bars, and on the Internet but never find *true* love. One possible explanation is that they never develop an understanding of what they seek. There are at least three basic types of love: *eros, philia,* and *agapé*.[1] The kind of love each person finds depends in part on his or her understanding of love and what motivates him or her to seek it.

Eros is self-serving and conditional. To a large extent, the attraction is based on physical attributes, and the participants enter the relationship without sufficient knowledge of (or regard for) each other's personality or needs. They readily accept each other's positive traits, yet they have little tolerance for negative traits as they emerge. The relationship is tolerated only as long as it makes the individuals feel good. Ultimately the relationship is doomed by the absence of a conscious decision to sustain the bond. While eros may function to preserve the species, it is unlikely to satisfy the psychological and partnering needs of both parties.

Philia is love that is mutually beneficial (e.g., shared rent, shared commuting between coworkers, etc.), and the parties usually have some familiarity with each other. Positive traits are readily accepted, and negative traits are tolerated—but only to a point. Should the negative traits pose too much of a problem, the commitment may dwindle and the relationship becomes threatened.

Agapé is based on honesty, trust, and selflessness. Each individual makes a conscious decision to accept the other unconditionally—positive and negative traits alike. The relationship is not marred by rudeness, envy, pride, or impatience.[2] Each party has genuine concern for the other, values the relationship, and exhibits kindness and forgiveness toward the other. There is mutual respect and an abiding hope for the future. It is an enduring love.

Agapé is akin to the unconditional love the creator has for us.[3] In spite of our disobedience, he does not forsake us. Instead he waits patiently for us to return to the covenantal relationship we established with him and comply with his commandments: to worship no other god (idols, money, fame, or influence), to love each other as he has loved us, and so on. Hoping to redeem us, he sent his only begotten son to deliver his word and show us the way to his kingdom. The son willingly laid down his life for the redemption of true believers. This is the kind of unselfish love agapé encompasses.[4] Spouses who possess such love remain true to their wedding vows.

Unconditional love extends well beyond romantic relationships. It is displayed when a passerby charges into a burning house to save the life of a stranger or when a soldier risks his or her life to save a comrade on the battlefield. Both the passerby and the soldier disregard the person's age, sex, race, and political affiliation. All that really matters is that the person in danger is also a child of God.

The ultimate expression of faith is to revere the Creator, keep his commandments, and emulate his unconditional love with regard to other people. Faith is more valuable than all the riches our secular world can bestow upon us; it is the way that leads to redemption and everlasting life in the kingdom.

A Love That Never Fails

In college I met a nice girl
And introduced myself to her.
With bright brown pupils set in pearl,
She caused my sound knees to falter.

I started a conversation,
While we went for a brief toddle.
She supplied witty narration
And strolled like a supermodel.

That night while we enjoyed dinner,
I became infatuated.
It was clear she was a winner—
My searching would be abated.

I wanted to say how I felt,
But thought it was a bit too soon.
Feelings were kept under my belt
Until a time more opportune.

We'd known each other forty days
When I told her I was smitten.
At first she gave me polite praise,
Then proceeded to enlighten.

She said my feelings were normal—
They came from physical appeal.
A short fling would be abysmal;
She wanted a more lasting deal.

We still went out with each other
And slowly became better friends.
I defied the urge to smother
And altered the prevailing winds.

We established brotherly love—
Of all her friends I was the best.
With time we fit like hand in glove—
That much she finally confessed.

Prudence brought greater acceptance—
Seize the good and abide the bad.
Our friendship acquired endurance,
But still could end and leave us sad.

Divine love is better by far,
Because it's unconditional.
It even persists from afar,
And its vast source is eternal.

At first I did not understand
How God's word would make us stronger.
To love like him is a command
That would make our love last longer.

We learned to be patient and kind
And refused to envy or boast.
With selfishness left far behind,
We wed before the Holy Ghost.

My best friend now for many years—
She is the wind that fills my sails.
Through thick and thin, laughter and tears,
We built a love that never fails.

Sea of Tranquility

After three months of ceaseless work,
I indulged in a valued perk.
I took a three-day weekend off;
My wife advised I not play golf.

Instead, we spent time at the beach
And watched the seagulls soar and screech.
Strolling together hand in hand,
Our feet soaked up warmth from the sand.

Sandpipers darted to and fro
As fast as their slim legs could go.
Sand crabs peeked from their beachfront holes
To watch pale tourists take their strolls.

The pounding surf reminded me
Of hidden power in the sea.
It buoyed surfers for a ride
On boards they worked with skill and pride.

At dusk I gave her a surprise—
A beach picnic before moonrise.
We spread out the picnic blanket
And took the meal from our basket.

With the summer sun sinking low,
Earth's star began to lose its glow.
Nightfall would debut a full moon
In a star-filled sky in mid-June.

Just as we washed our hands with soap,
A man readied his telescope
Atop a bridge over the dune.
The bright full moon would appear soon.

We did not have a lot of time
To race across the sand and grime.
We climbed the steps and reached the bridge
Bearing two lobsters for his fridge.

He was delighted to have guests
And rushed to fill our drink requests.
He shared with us his stargazing—
We hoped it would be amazing.

He spoke of his late wife with pride;
She spent five decades by his side.
They often observed the moonrise—
It's more romantic than sunrise.

They shared a love that would not end—
He was her guy and her best friend.
And when her health was very grave,
They kept the faith that made them brave.

Just prior to her final rest,
They prayed for just one more request:
To meet for a grand rendezvous
At a place they both loved and knew.

There she would wait for him to come;
He was her love and lifelong chum.
From there they would seek the kingdom
To praise the father of wisdom.

Just as he finished his story,
The moon rose in all its glory.
We were both very excited
To see the place he'd just cited.

He focused on the moon's surface
To find the spot that was their ace.
At the Sea of Tranquility,
They'd meet, then seek eternity.

We looked and felt that she was there,
Watching over her mate with care.
They managed to make their love thrive,
Because her spirit was alive.

Since then we have not been the same—
Enthralled by their eternal flame.
Tears of joy trickle from our eyes
Each time we see a full moon rise.

Chasing Love in Cyberspace

I wandered through life day by day;
Somehow I could not find my way.
I filled my life with constant work—
And I was just a warehouse clerk.

One day a friend pulled me aside
And hinted I should find a bride.
I earnestly gave it a whirl,
But still I could not find a girl.

He recommended cyberspace,
Where women dwell from every place.
He said I'd surely find a date,
With luck she would become my mate.

I logged onto the Internet—
It seemed to be my surest bet.
The choice of girls was very vast,
Surely I'd find a girlfriend fast.

The hours of search turned into days
And did not end my lonely ways.
At last I asked the man above,
"Please help me find someone to love."

One sunny day my cyber mail
Contained a note—her name was Gail.
I read it and thought instantly
I'd found a girlfriend, finally.

We soon arranged an online chat;
She sent her photo to look at.
We spoke of children—maybe two,
But Gail's hometown was Timbuktu.

Although it was just cyber love,
I thought she was sent from above.
I had someone to call my own,
And yet I still felt all alone.

I went to church one rainy day
And got down on my knees to pray.
"Please give me just one girl to love—
Just as you pair the mourning dove."

The very instant I was done,
I saw a girl—a lovely one.
She too was praying on her knees,
"Grant me true love dear father, please."

She met a guy in cyberspace
But thought it was a scary place.
Although she felt alone and blue,
She claimed to live in Timbuktu.

Quickly I asked, "Is your name Gail?"
Then told her about her e-mail.
We floundered out in cyberspace
But triumphed in that holy place.

She was a queen who made me king,
And now she wears my wedding ring.
The story made the preacher laugh—
The way I found my better half.

Into the Wind

I point my bike into the wind
Then rush to her—she is my friend.
She howls above the engine's roar
And gives the lift that lets me soar.

Each time I ride into the wind,
It sets me free and I pretend.
Sometimes I leave the earth below
And caw just like a raucous crow.

I travel light, I travel fast,
And think of good times from the past.
Relieved of woes that fill my head,
I hunger for the road ahead.

I roll like thunder on two wheels—
Elated by how good it feels.
I see the beauty of this land,
All fashioned by the master's hand.

I'm grateful for the time I spend,
Riding alone into the wind.
Sometimes while sitting on my perch,
Come answers to a life of search.

At dusk—with sunlight sinking low—
I marvel in the afterglow.
Riding at night beneath the stars,
I ponder love and life on Mars.

The sunrise brings a brand new day,
As I cross the Chesapeake Bay.
By then I'm one with my machine
On the way to St. Augustine.

While riding on the Outer Banks,
I take some time to give God thanks.
Then off I go past Hilton Head—
An awesome place from all I've read.

While far removed from cold and snow,
I revel in the warm airflow.
The wind reminds me as I roam
Of past rides to our winter home.

Fond thoughts of her and our snug brood
Makes me smile and livens my mood.
I'm just a romantic snowbird
Riding without his lost lovebird.

Some fear for me because I ride,
But from the wind I will not hide.
I know she's waiting 'round the bend,
That's why I ride into the wind.

FAITH

Humans have long felt subservient to a higher power, but we developed confusion about the source of that power. Some thought it emanated from visible sources, and so they paid homage to earthly objects (mountains, trees, or idols). Others bowed down to heavenly bodies (the sun, moon, or stars). Still others gazed out beyond the discernible heavenly bodies toward an unseen deity in the void of outer space. They believed the unseen spiritual being was—and always will be—the one and only true God. They credited him with creating both the heavens and earth. Belief in an unseen creator is the essence of *faith*.[5]

Religion is a set of beliefs held by a group of people concerning the creation and oversight of the universe by a superhuman power. The group usually submits itself to leadership by an individual or a governing council.

Three of the major religions—Christianity, Judaism, and Islam—share a common God. The origin of all three can be traced to a single predecessor—Abraham.[6] He was deemed righteous by the creator because of his unwavering faith.

The manner in which the three religions worship God may vary, but the creator remains unchanged. Considering how he established a relationship with Abraham based on Abraham's righteousness, it's safe to assume that the three religions should also promote righteous living and reverence for the creator. I firmly believe that all of Abraham's offspring will be judged by the fervor of their faith and how they act upon that faith.[7] While I advocate being affiliated with a religion, it is unlikely that merely belonging to a religion guarantees favor with the creator.

Each religion should set the worshiper on the path to righteous living by outlining the creator's expectations of each individual. These expectations were communicated through Abraham and other believers whose lives were affected by divine intervention. Their godly encounters are recorded in the Bible, the Torah, and the Koran.

Parents are instrumental in the spiritual development of their children. They should read to them from the holy book of their respective religion and take them to their place of worship. As spiritually mature adults, it is crucial for parents and members of the extended family to do their best to serve as role models of righteous living for their children. In an environment of love, surrounded by faithful individuals, the child matures into a faithful adult. It is then up to the young adult to sustain his or her faith and decide how to act upon it in daily life. One must be diligent so that the concerns of the secular world do not trump the faith that tethers the individual to the creator.

How we live indicates who (God) or what (money, power, notoriety, invincibility) we worship.[8] A life consumed by the pursuit of material things will prove to be an exercise in futility. After all, "things" do not accompany us into the afterlife; instead they remain behind for others to enjoy. A more prudent life is one that is guided by faith and results in our being deemed righteous by the creator.

All of us should take to heart the wisdom imparted by King Solomon. Near the end of his life, he concluded, "Fear God and keep his commandments—for this is the whole duty of man" (Eccles. 12:13).[9]

Children of Abraham

Three key religions of the world
Share Abraham as their father.
But judging by the insults hurled,
The bloodline has lost its tether.

Each has its own holiest place
And will not pray with distant kin.
When will Abraham's sons embrace?
Their bitterness is wearing thin.

Hebrews extol the Western Wall—[10]
A prized Second Temple relic.[11]
It's also where Muslims recall
A midnight ride that's symbolic.

Buraq the steed was tethered there,
After a grand trip from Mecca.[12]
The wall is for both groups to share—
As kinsmen share healing yucca.[13]

The Christians have their sacred shrine—
Church of the Holy Sepulcher.[14]
There, at Calvary they share wine
To honor their God-sent teacher.

The time has come to heed the call
To have a common pilgrimage.[15]
For it was God who made us all
To reflect his *loving* image.

O Jerusalem, serve your God![16]
He blessed us all through Abraham,
Then gave his offspring sacred sod
To share—not make our brothers scram.

Power of the Word

In the beginning was the word;
Through it the universe was made.[17]
That's why I've commonly deferred
To all that God and son have bade.

The word directs my stint on earth[18]
And reels me in when prone to stray.
I'm ever mindful of its worth
And thank God for it when I pray.

Sometimes the cares of earthly life
Drown out the word that counsels me.
But like the playing of the fife,
The word resounds and sets me free.

It's good to know I'm not alone;
I learned that I'm a blessed host.
Through God's word he has made it known
My body bears the Holy Ghost.[19]

The word always keeps me aware
Of the love he has for us all.
Mercy is offered with great care
To right us whenever we fall.

I'm no longer crippled by strife,
But turn to his word for comfort.[20]
It is the road map for my life
That guides me to his peaceful fort.

The word gives me purpose and hope—
Knowing his kingdom is to come.
With that in mind I've learned to cope
And move to the beat of his drum.

Life is finally making sense
Because I've found divine meaning.
His word calms me when I am tense—
I relish his intervening.

As I fade into the sunset
And slip from the thundering herd,
For me there will be no regret—
My fate rests squarely on his word.[21]

Right Always Wins

We all serve a higher power,
And doing good brings him delight.
Vile acts done with Satan's glower
Angers God because they're not right.

It doesn't matter who we are—
All people reap just what they sow.[22]
It's up to us to raise the bar,
Dealing with either friend or foe.

He who sets out seeking revenge
Should always prepare two coffins.
The act he sets out to avenge
Can destroy the soul—if he sins.

Forego swift gratification
If it causes us to stumble.
Seek instead, justification
That leaves us righteous and humble.

Our foes are neither brave nor strong
When they resort to dreadful sins.
Don't be tempted by acts of wrong,
For in the end right *always* wins.

A Legacy of His Word

His word is like a precious stone
That has value to everyone.
We all desire it for our own
Before our life on earth is done.

Men of the cloth are like shepherds—
Each does his best to guide his flock.
They deliver God's spoken words—
Each one as solid as a rock.

When one of the flock goes astray,
It brings him back into the fold.
Then in a very gentle way,
It has him do what God has told.

Loving parents teach right from wrong
To kids who are their legacy.
They impart words that guide lifelong
And prove they have adequacy.

The word serves as our guiding light
To help each of us find our way.
Through them we learn to do what's right
Instead of doing as we may.

The elders in the family,
Correct a kid who's misbehaved.
Armed with the word they readily
Teach the way that renders him saved.

On the day when we close our eyes,
We'll see the one to whom we pray.
He will proclaim we won the prize—
Because God's word showed us the way.

The Duty of Man

Chasing our American dreams
Is all there is, or so it seems.
While we buy name brands to adorn,
Children die on Africa's horn.

Making money to flaunt and spend
Is futile, as is chasing wind.
We gain the world and then we die;
Our spoils stay for others to buy.

We hail advancements made by man
And give no thought to God's great plan.
We search space for alien life
And shun earth's famine, drought, and strife.

Oh God, when will you intervene
Or send once more your Nazarene?
He brought your word to help us all
So we won't sin, falter, or fall.

God said to all, as if on cue,
"This is the land I gave to you
To rule and take dominion of —
Without intrusion from above."[23]

Good stewards we have failed to be,
Though God instructed lovingly.
We pillage and ruin mother earth,
Although we understand her worth.

Christ promised to return one day.
Exactly when, he did not say.[24]
On that solemn day he will judge
Just how we spent our earthly trudge.

So come and preach—you faithful few,
The truth that King Solomon knew.
Obeying God since time began
Has been the whole duty of man.

Keep Jerusalem Unified

I pray for dear Jerusalem
To keep her whole and draped in peace.
In the past they called her Salem,
When warring factions would not cease.

Three sects claim the holy city
And compete for God's holy site.
It would be a senseless pity
To desecrate her in a fight.

It's claimed by each vain demigod
Who seeks his own vile agenda.
Jerusalem was picked by God
As *his* earthly hacienda.[25]

Jerusalem is hallowed sod—
It is not ours to divvy up.
All faiths should wear just one ephod
And drink from the same sacred cup.

Festival of Tabernacles
Is a time when *all* celebrate.
So heed prophetic oracles
And let the nations congregate.

Salem is where we worship him—[26]
He is the potter, we are clay.[27]
Our future will be very grim
If she is razed by foolish fray.

Religions should preach words of love
And praise our God through pomp and hymn.
They risk spurning the holy dove
Should they carve up Jerusalem.

Before I Cross Over

My trip on earth is very short,
And it has been a bumpy ride.
Sometimes I yearn for the comfort
Residing on the other side.

But there is still much left to do
Before I'm called to cross over.
My accomplishments are so few
Because I live as a rover.

Perhaps I should donate more time—
Tutoring kids so they can soar.
I should end my self-serving crime
And do much more to help the poor.

There are times I could share my faith;
Instead I cower in my shoes.
I often hide my inner wraith
By holding onto his good news.

So every time I kneel to pray,
I plead to give me inner strength."
Then I could spend each given day
Working for him at greater length.

I do not know the time or day—
Life fades as fast as wild clover.
I'll act today without delay
To shine before I cross over.

HOPE

Time seemed to move very slowly in early childhood, only to speed up once formal education began. While preoccupied with learning the basics, I began to feel parental and societal pressures to achieve high marks. I admired and sought to emulate the academic prowess, social maturity, and competitive spirit of the upperclassmen. I also thought it would be great to participate in activities enjoyed by older pupils, such as skating, scouting, team sports, and so forth.

In junior high school, it seemed it would take forever to reach high school—the time when most teens obtained their driver's licenses. Driving would afford me some semblance of independence and enable me to go to movies, the mall, and friends' homes without being transported by my parents or older siblings.

Similarly in high school I yearned to go off to college and be on my own—though I still expected financial support from my parents. I regarded college as the final frontier for academics, social maturation, and honing my competitive spirit. My class ranking at commencement would be the main determinant in securing an awesome job when I entered the competitive workforce (a.k.a. the rat race).

I eventually finished undergraduate, graduate, and postgraduate schools and secured a job. Though I was not saddled with large student loan payments, I had to support myself and my family. Suddenly my brood and I were bona fide consumers in stiff competition with our neighbors—the dreaded "Joneses."

Financial institutions deluged us with unsolicited credit card applications, offers for home mortgage loans with adjustable rates, and no-down-payment auto loans. Product advertisements were hurled at us on television, by landline and cell phone, via snail mail and e-mail, in newspapers, on billboards, in movie theaters, and in public urinals.

Our tech-savvy kids began to exhibit diminished writing and language skills as a result of endless hours spent texting in an alien language.[28] We learned that our gas-guzzling SUVs and energy-sapping homes were injuring the environment, yet we didn't want to change our lifestyle or push for legislation that might hurt the economy. Our childhoods, it seemed, were all about getting a good education to get a good job so we could become ravenous consumers. We became free-enterprise saps—lusting for the latest gadgets. Gradually, we began to question the logic of it all and searched for greater meaning in life—meaning that fostered hope.

Hope is a feeling of expectation for the future. It provides optimism and inspires us to persevere. Faith offers the greatest reason to have hope.[29] Unwavering belief in an unseen creator provides a reason for optimism.

We now turn our focus away from the realm where humankind has stewardship and direct our faith toward an infinite universe where God presides.[30] We are more meticulous in our efforts to obey his commandments—especially the one to love one another (including the Joneses) just as he loves us. We also strive to become better stewards of Earth.

Life takes on a higher meaning because of God's promise of eternal bliss for the faithful. My family and I view life on Earth as preparatory school for entry into the kingdom—the requirements for which are outlined in the scriptures. Thus faith provides an abiding hope that sustains us through our fleeting corporeal life. Through faith we are deemed righteous, righteousness leads to salvation and a perpetual spiritual life in God's kingdom. Surely there is no greater reason to have hope.

Thank Goodness for Hope

Life is a roller coaster ride—
Sometimes I'm up, sometimes I'm down.
I try to take it all in stride
And try hard not to cast a frown.

I can't resist family time
And being surrounded by love.
We raid the beach in summertime
And romp beneath the sun above.

When caught up in a thunderstorm,
We see how trees gleam when it rains.
He flaunts a rainbow to inform
That he is God and always reigns.

Each passing year is filled with change,
And challenges are abundant.
When life gets tough and downright strange,
I know God's love remains constant.

I live by faith and not by sight;[31]
God guides my living with his word.
And when I wander from what's right,
I'm saved by his loving shepherd.

One day when my journey is done,
I will relent to blissful sleep.
He vows to be the only one
In whose hands my spirit will keep.

The Motherland

Africa gave birth to all men
In Eden's beautiful garden.
But callousness consumes our hearts—
So the end for Africa starts.

We all forsake the motherland,
While drought turns fertile soil to sand.[32]
We watch its native people die
And we refuse to pause or cry.

The problem is so serious,
And we're not even curious.
Their troubles have not reached us yet,
So why should we become upset?

Africa is a warning sign
That life on Earth is less than fine.[33]
Though disasters spread at slow pace
They find their way to every place.

There is only one solution—
We must reduce our pollution.
But we're a nation hooked on oil;
If we don't change the seas will boil.

A frog won't pollute his own pond—
A home of which he's very fond.
Woes affect all inhabitants
And spread to unborn descendants.

Mankind's' domicile is the Earth—
A place of ever-shrinking girth.
All life is interconnected—
A fact that's often rejected.

For the sake of all our children,
It's time to unite as brethren;
Then, pledge to take a noble stand
That gives hope to our motherland.

We Are One

Some people in our fragile world
Ignore events that have unfurled.[34]
They have the means to carry on—
Though doom lurks on the horizon.

They flourish high above the fray,
While others struggle day by day.
And as they enjoy a pampered life,
The earth has slowly filled with strife.

They expand their carbon footprint,
While others struggle to pay rent.
With means to make a difference,
They thrive on sheer indifference.[35]

Some strive to reach the arid moon,
While life on Earth may vanish soon.[36]
With gazes fixed on outer space—
Their focus is on the wrong place.

The earth has had a climate shift;
Abuse has set all life adrift.
Earth ails from man's activity
To raise his productivity.

Appointed stewards by our God,
We pollute air, water, and sod.
So now we want to conquer space
After damaging our birthplace.

No wonder our kids cannot cope—
We give them no reason to hope.
If not for us, then change for them;
The earth is our most precious gem.

Let's heed our duty to protect,
And treat the earth with more respect.
We have all been placed on notice
To mend the earth with fond service.

Regardless if we're rich or poor,
We all will knock on heaven's door.
In honor of both God and son,
Let's care for earth, for we are one.[37]

CHARITY

Charity is love for humanity expressed by rendering aid to others. Sometimes charity can be self-serving—as when benevolence is shown publicly for self-promotion.[38] Providing aid can be mutually beneficial, as when people donate to a charity for tax relief or when companies show goodwill to increase their customer base.

Charity can also be unconditional, especially when it is rendered anonymously.[39] Occasionally it may require some measure of personal sacrifice, as when someone donates blood, bone marrow, or an organ to a stranger. In rare cases it may result in a person laying down his or her life for another. Aid workers may risk their lives in war zones, or a passerby may charge an armed assailant to save a complete stranger.

Demonstrating our love for others through charity affirms that we love the creator who first loved us. He commands us to love one another as he loves us and as we love ourselves. Anyone who hates his neighbor yet professes to love God is a liar. John, the apostle of Jesus, expresses this notion in the Bible (1 John 4:19–21). He explains that it is inconceivable that a person could love a God he hasn't seen yet hate the neighbor he has seen.

The Koran, the Torah, and the Bible all contain some version of the golden rule: *do unto others as you would have them do unto you*. Even so there is discord among the three religions that pay homage to the very same God.

If all of us—both individuals and religious groups—performed more charitable acts, Earth would truly be a different place.[40] Poverty, health care inequities, and disparities in education would be greatly reduced.

We are actively developing a global economy, yet a stalemate has occurred in our efforts to attain global peace, achieve nuclear disarmament, reduce global warming, and ensure human rights. If nations diverted progressively larger amounts of military spending toward charitable acts for friends and enemies alike, it would be mutually beneficial, and heaven and earth would rejoice.

I occasionally reflect on the biblical book of Jonah. God commanded the prophet Jonah to go to Nineveh (the capital city of Israel's enemy, the Assyrian empire) and warn its citizens of impending destruction if they continued their evil ways.[41] Instead, Jonah hid from God, intending to allow the destruction of his enemy. After suffering unfathomable horrors, Jonah finally complied with God's instructions. He convinced the city to repent, and Nineveh was spared. This is but one example of God's love for our enemies and his compassion toward *all* nations.[42]

Charity is not just an expression of the love we have for our fellow humans—it is also the realization that the creator made all of us in his own image. If we love him, then we love the person in the mirror, the individuals in our household, those in our neighborhood, and all members of our global community. If all God's people understood this, there would be no need for nuclear weapons. We would also solve the problems of world hunger, health care, and global warming for the sake of all humanity.

Of faith, hope, and love, the greatest of is love, for it eclipses the previous two and persists long after faith and hope are no more.[43] The creator is the originator of love and has promised life in his kingdom for those who truly love him as well as their fellow humans.

Loathing the Enemy

Sometimes I reflect on Jonah,
Who tried to hide from Jehovah.[44]
When told to preach to Nineveh,
He chose instead to disobey.

He felt entirely no pity
For his foe's capital city.
Slated for divine destruction—
Why give her righteous instruction?

He thought grace was just for Hebrews
And sought refuge among ship crews.[45]
He chose a ship bound for Tarshish,
But ended up inside a fish.

Jonah forsook his selfish plan
And placed all in the master's hand.
Forced from the fish into the light,
He abandoned his senseless flight.

With God's help Jonah understood
The worth of doing as he should.
He informed the dire Ninevites
And they placed heaven in their sights.[46]

He learned that God cares for his foes,
And schemes to purge them lead to woes.
They learned that God's love is ample—
Thanks to Jonah's strange example.

Darfur Is Our Shame

No longer can I bear the shame
Or hide the source from whence it came.
It came from where mankind was born,
Far away on Africa's horn.

The raging horror in Sudan
Cries out to every decent man.[47]
Although action is overdue,
There's still time to mount a rescue.

The UN will not keep the peace,
And so the killing will not cease.[48]
It tolerates vast genocide
And ignores vile rapes countrywide.

While members play their politics,
More people die as the clock ticks.
The UN has turned a blind eye
To all the people yet to die.

America must take the lead
To help a people fraught with need.
We must not wait or pass the buck—
This is a cause we cannot duck.[49]

Our leader—from his safe sedan—
Rides out the problems in Sudan.
Evil reigns when a righteous hand
Fails to rise up and take a stand.[50]

Rise up moral majority,
And reveal your fidelity.
Rally your political base
To write or call and plead their case.

Decisive action is a must
For all who chant, "In God we trust."
Our goodness suffers at its core
If we do nothing for Darfur.

Pro-life Saves All Children

A child does not ask to be born
Or choose the home it will adorn.
They are precious gifts from above
That bring forth our most cherished love.

All kids deserve a valid chance
To live their lives without hindrance.
We're like no other animal—
Our potential is maximal.

Some people say they are pro-life,[51]
Yet turn their backs to children's strife.
They deem life precious before birth,
But afterward it has no worth.

Poor mothers lack prenatal care
And live with hunger and despair.[52]
Their kids are born with low birth weight,
Which raises the infant death rate.[53]

Too many kids are uninsured
And suffer ills that can be cured.
It seems pro-life is just a ploy
That hollow candidates employ.

Politicians have great health care
Paid by the poor—it's just not fair.[54]
The country needs health care reform,
It's time for Congress to transform.

Third-world children lack clean water,
Which causes their health to falter.
Millions die from diarrhea[55]
And Pro-life folks don't shed a tear.

Prompted by big coal companies,
We poison the land, sky, and seas.
Kids need a clean environment,
Yet we destroy the firmament.

Pro-life is not just rhetoric—
It's a call to be heroic.
I challenge all pro-life brethren
To defend *all* of God's children.

Face of the Homeless

I used to avoid the homeless
By jaywalking across the street.[56]
How could I have been so heartless,[57]
So much has been laid at my feet?[58]

One day my brother lost his job[59]
And decided he would vanish.
There wasn't time for me to sob—
Finding him was my only wish.

My torment went on for three years
Until I got a doctor's call.
I thought he would confirm my fears
And braced myself against a wall.

He said my brother became sick
And did not have health insurance.[60]
His pride was just too great to kick,
So he did not seek assistance.

The homeless aren't worthless creatures[61]
Who yield to drugs and liquor stills.
Some of them are laid-off teachers
Or people swamped by health care bills.

Let's not forget the homeless kids[62]
Who walk the streets with a parent.
Let's pray we do not hit the skids
And can't afford to pay the rent.

Health care should be a human right[63]
Since we all are mortal creatures.
It's time to end the health care fight—
Our lives have too many pressures.

Anyone could fall penniless
With only barren streets to pace.
No more can I shun the homeless—
Since each one dons my brother's face.

Ode to My Neighbor

I asked Dad, "Who is my neighbor?"[64]
He said they may not look like me.
Some come from a distant harbor,
But share a common destiny.

Too often we think of *neighbor*
As those who live next door to us.
We shun those who do field labor
And those who drive the city bus.

We spurn folks from across the sea
Who may not speak our native tongue.
It took some time for me to see
That neighbors are truly far-flung.

I realized that I've been wrong
To befriend just those I favor.
And so I wrote this simple song
For people who are my neighbor.

"We all are made from the same mold
And share the same aspirations.
This idea may seem new or bold,
Yet valid for generations.

"I'll grant both love and charity
To any neighbor fraught with need.
My faith is only vanity
If I perform no earthly deed."[65]

"I also pledge to free myself
By helping those who are oppressed.
Treating all neighbors as oneself
Is the way to be truly blessed."[66]

Remember the Downtrodden

Our views on humane services
Suggest our vision is impaired.
We squint like hapless novices
Whenever our wealth should be shared.

Camels will pass through a needle
Before the rich see paradise.
They swindle, hustle, and wheedle
To reap more cash and merchandise.

The rich crave another tax break
And snub socialized medicine.
Hoarding the wealth for their own sake,
Makes stinginess look just like sin.

The rich neglect our nation's poor,[67]
As though their plight does not matter.
It speaks to what lies at their core
When they spew self-serving chatter.

The orphan needs a stable home[68]
Surrounded by nurture and love.[69]
Although they have a wild genome,
They are loved by our God above.

Towns discharge their mentally ill
To avoid giving chronic care.[70]
They are sent to the streets to mill
With barely anything to wear.

Most widows have a heavy heart
And live alone to battle grief.[71]
The rest of us should do our part
To visit them and bring relief.

Many lives have been ripped apart
And their troubled minds are sodden.
For heaven's sake open your heart,
And reach out to the downtrodden.

THE EARTH

Earth is the third planet in our solar system. It lies near the end of an arm extending from a spiral galaxy called the Milky Way. Humankind is but one species among millions that inhabit the planet. We are thought to be the only creatures that possess a high degree of intelligence and the ability to reason. We can differentiate between right and wrong, learn from our mistakes, and plan for a better future. Thus the Almighty endowed us with a smattering of his traits, though we often fail to utilize them wisely.

A few thousand years ago, 12 percent of Earth's surface was covered by rain forest. Today rain forest covers 2 percent.[72] Half of all animal species on Earth are dependent on rain forests.[73] Worldwide, eighty thousand acres of rain forest are lost each day.[74]

Actively growing trees convert carbon dioxide into oxygen through a process called photosynthesis.[75] Tropical forests absorb about 18 percent of all carbon dioxide released into the air from fossil fuels. When trees die the wood decays and the carbon dioxide they absorbed is deposited on the forest floor. Deforestation and burning of the trees and underbrush release sequestered carbon products back into the air.[76]

Fossil fuels are formed naturally from decaying or buried organisms. The process requires hundreds of millions of years and yields substances such as methane, petroleum, and anthracite coal. Combustion of fossil fuels provides energy for humankind's endeavors and releases about twenty-one billion tons of carbon dioxide per year. Only half of that amount can be removed annually by nature. Fossil fuel combustion releases other by-products into the atmosphere, including nitric oxide and sulfur dioxide. Both compounds combine with atmospheric water and return to Earth in the form of acid rain.[77]

Coal-burning power plants also release mercury into the environment and are responsible for half of the mercury pollution.[78]

Mercury has contaminated fish around the globe—both saltwater and freshwater species.[79]

Simultaneously commercial fishing is depleting the oceans of fish supplies and has caused catastrophic changes in marine biodiversity. Fishing trawlers drag nets across the ocean floor and trap or kill essentially all fish, mollusks, and other creatures they encounter. Nets devastate coral reefs and transform the ocean's floor into mud. Reefs are essential breeding beds for hundreds of species.[80]

Long-line and other forms of commercial fishing have taken the population of tuna and swordfish to the brink of extinction. The ocean ecosystem has also been greatly disturbed by a devastating reduction in the shark population due to commercial fishing.[81]

The Creator formed the universe—including Earth and all of its life-forms. He created humankind and authorized us to protect Earth's species and manage natural resources responsibly. We have been derelict in these tasks. Even after realizing our mistakes, we have not modified our behavior to diminish the deleterious impact human activity has on other species, the atmosphere, plant life, the oceans, and future generations. Human beings have allowed commercial pursuits to trump intelligent management of the ecological systems that are essential to the survival of *all* species.

We have chosen to ignore divine guidance and risk *everything* in our pursuit of wealth. Perhaps it is not in *God* we trust—instead it is the dollar we revere.

The Blue Planet

My home lies in the Milky Way,
A star-studded spiral array.[82]
The neighborhood glows very bright
To every stargazer's delight.

Near the tip of a spiral arm
Our blue planet glows with great charm.
It has two poles that glisten white
To reflect its star's brilliant light.[83]

Earth's oceans yield a blue color;
White clouds add contrasting pallor.[84]
Terra firma frames the waters,
And trees act as Earth's air filters.[85]

But our blue planet is changing—
Its polar ice caps are melting.[86]
The trees are not as numerous—
A sign of something onerous.[87]

Some surface locales glow all night,
Produced by artificial light.[88]
Smog covers strange concrete jungles;
A sign of enduring bungles

What has gone wrong on planet Earth
To cause problems of such broad girth?[89]
It must lack intelligent life,
Or else it would correct such strife.

As the earth's colors fade away,
Her neighbors have begun to say:
"The galaxy will miss the hue
Of its sole planet colored blue."

Razing Mother Earth

We love to drive an SUV[90]
And crave things we see on TV.[91]
We all waste electricity,[92]
And share a great duplicity.

From coal that fuels our luxury,
We lace Earth's fish with mercury.
It also emits CO_2
That ruins the air for me and you.

Trees take CO_2 from the air;
No other method can compare.
Countless trees continue to fall
Just to build another strip mall.[93]

Due to a huge climatic change,
More storms reach a critical range.[94]
Some ask why kids depend on dope
As we destroy their every hope.

God gave Earth for man to protect,
But we treat her with gross neglect.
Will God have mercy on us all
When he takes his final roll call?

Humans thrive on sheer arrogance
And won't confront their ignorance.[95]
Human endeavor has no worth
If we keep razing Mother Earth.

Clean Coal

The planet needs clean energy
To ease the lives of everyone.
The source should work in synergy
And not cause harm to anyone.

There's endless talk about clean coal[96]
To cut our need for foreign crude.[97]
It will help us achieve our goal—
According to some TV dude.

Coal fills the earth with mercury
And finds its way into our fish.
The metal threatens injury[98]
Each time we eat a seafood dish.

Coal leaves a large carbon footprint—
A fact that liars can't cajole.[99]
Man's time on Earth will soon be spent
Unless we stop igniting coal.

So end the talk about clean coal;[100]
It's fanciful technology.[101]
We cannot tolerate the toll
It has on Earth's ecology.

God's Green Earth

I watch as busy honeybees
Take pollen from the lily field.
Sometimes I lower to my knees
And marvel at their tiny yield.

I relish walking through the woods
To reach a cold stream filled with fish.
Through generations of childhoods
It provides kids their first sunfish.

Amid a rolling field of wheat,
I listen to the rustling heads.
The clamor is an awesome treat,
Like angels thrashing where man treads.

New England's foliage in the fall
Is painted by the master's brush.
The bright colors remind us all—
Each phase of life should bring a rush.

In awe of winter's wonderland,
I dash to the nearest ski slope.
The pure white landscape is so grand,
It conjures heaven and brings hope.

For me spring is an awesome time—
It ushers in nature's rebirth.
But due to mankind's senseless crime,
Pollution threatens God's green earth.

My grandkids may not have seasons
Due to rampant global warming.
Of all the possible reasons,
A lack of will seems so damning.

Our fathers built this great nation
And vastly increased their net worth.
But the greatest generation
Did not stress care for God's green earth.

Here's the Beef

We all relish the hamburger,
A valued American treat.[102]
To relieve our pangs of hunger,
We must rely on other meat.

The ever-growing need for beef
Demands countless herds of cattle.[103]
They cause a stench that begs relief
And won't resolve with glib tattle.[104]

Methane speeds up global warming,
And cattle are a major source.[105]
To stop our climate from changing,
We must alter our dinner course.

If we thin our herds of cattle,
It will help the earth's atmosphere.
From Miami to Seattle,
Let's make our message loud and clear.

We'll start by saying, "Here's the beef!
Methane poses a global threat.
Avoiding beef will save us grief—
Ongoing use will cause regret."

Reducing Our Carbon Footprints

Many scientists advocate
Man should shrink his carbon footprint.[106]
When fossil fuels incinerate,
They harm the earth's environment.

Soon there will be electric cars
Recharged by coal-fired power plants.[107]
This may thrill automotive czars,
But it's not cool, despite their rants.

Both gasoline and coal pollute,
Causing our Earth great injury.
Although coal will save lots of loot,
It taints the earth with mercury.

One solution we overlook
Is slowing the human birth-rate.[108]
It would improve global outlook
Since less footprints would help our fate.

Many of us neuter our pets
To control the population.
We take them to our local vets
To solve a dire situation.

With rising human density
Other species feel our pressure.[109]
More people live in poverty,
And we all become less secure.

Our country touts its leading role
In solving intricate problems.
Yet we won't promote birth control[110]
To save Earth's critical systems.

The Alaskan Refuge

The soaring price of gasoline
Has caused a rush to intervene.[111]
We're told supplies are very huge[112]
Up in the Alaskan refuge.[113]

Some say life there won't be disturbed[114]
Although Earth's ozone is perturbed.
The frozen tundra fades away,[115]
And glaciers there melt day by day.[116]

Hydrocarbons from ages past
Burn in the cars we drive so fast.
The exhaust harms the atmosphere
And threatens all that we hold dear.[117]

We need to find much cleaner fuels
Before Earth fills with human pules.
So let our great scientists probe[118]
To find safe fuels to save our globe.

Ignore bribed leaders and the rich
Who try to sell their lying pitch.
We must resist their subterfuge
To drill the Alaskan refuge.[119]

The Vanishing Snows of Kilimanjaro

My heart has a looming sorrow
Over Mount Kilimanjaro.[120]
She is dying from man's abuse—
And simply there is no excuse.

Both desert and lush rain forest
Flourished beneath her snowy crest.
She bore both plant life and wildlife
So lavishly and free of strife.

Her snows formed life-sustaining streams
That shimmered in God's bright sunbeams.
The Chagga natives were the key
That kept life there in harmony.[121]

Then coffee-growing dealmakers
Displaced the Chagga caretakers.[122]
Now no one bears her lofty cause
Or defends her life without pause.[123]

So brash loggers go and strip her,[124]
While climbers ascend and conquer.
If only Ernest Hemingway
Were here to fight for her today.

Harming Mount Kilimanjaro
Proves our minds are vile and narrow.
All climate zones are found on her—[125]
If she dies Earth too will falter.

We know it makes our future bleak
To have snow melt upon her peak.[126]
Yet we keep burning fossil fuels
That thaw her glacial molecules.

Her future is so onerous;
It is a sign for all of us.
Man can view his world tomorrow
Atop Mount Kilimanjaro.[127]

POLITICS

Politics concerns itself with the process by which groups compete for power or leadership in order to influence the affairs of the state. Ideally the process should serve the common good of constituents and not cater to the elite.

An effective political system demands that voters remain informed and engaged to ensure that competing political groups remain relevant. Voters should actively influence their party's platform through local convention delegates. Passive lifetime membership as a registered supporter of any party results in irrelevant platforms.[128] Voter passivity[129] and unhinged campaign financing have allowed the American political system to become adulterated by undue influence from political action committees (PACs), lobbyists, and elitists. Obscene amounts of money are funneled into the coffers of government officials in exchange for easy access and favorable influence.

An especially dangerous recent development is the formation of leadership PACs by congressmen.[130] It is a loophole in campaign financing that allows candidates to accumulate hundreds of thousands of dollars from special interest groups. In effect politicians are able to create virtual slush funds that enable them to lead lavish lifestyles above and beyond what is afforded by their salaries.

Unbridled greed and influence peddling have disenfranchised constituents and transformed elected officials into emissaries for their major donors.[131] This arrangement tarnishes the spirit in which the founding fathers established our democratic government and dishonors those who fight and die to defend it. Politicians have subverted our government *of the people, by the people, for the people.*[132] What is left is a government of the people, by the people, that serves special interests.

"In God We Trust" is inscribed on the face of our currency. But politicians' lust for the dollar has become akin to idol worship—the root of all political evil. Such money worship and the

failure of Congress to "regulate" financial institutions contributed to the financial meltdown that nearly ran the nation (as
well as the global economy) into the proverbial ditch.[133] Even
so the rich have become superrich, while an alarming number
among the masses experience the despair of unemployment
and homelessness.

Members of Congress rely on special interests to give them
perks and to finance their continuous campaigns.[134] Voters have
been reduced to clueless saps who cast votes only after candidates spend indecent amounts of money to influence their votes.
When conflicts of interest exist—due to stock ownership or campaign contributions—rather than recuse themselves, officials cast
their votes, benefit themselves and reward their contributors.[135]

The time has come to end the adulterous relationship elected
officials enjoy with their contributors, some of whom they regulate and oversee.[136] Their infidelity has eroded public confidence
in the political process.[137] The situation will improve only when voters insist on term limits and take advantage of recall elections to
remove immoral officials.

Constituents must band together and resist being polarized
by politicians. Voters should also remove their names from the
rolls of political parties (keep them guessing), demand effective
campaign finance reform, and if necessary form grassroots parties. In addition they should utilize write-in campaigns, engage
in public protests, insist on disclosure of conflicts of interest, and
hold firm to our motto In *God* We Trust—not in politicians who sell
themselves for money and lack the morals to reform.

Sidelining Politics

I asked a workmate for a date;
She sought *vital* information.
One key factor would seal our fate—
My party affiliation.

Most times I voted Democrat;
Yet, I was an American.
She seemed like an aristocrat
And a loyal Republican.

She pressed me to give an answer;
I had a fifty-fifty chance.
Being an accomplished dancer,
I cut a move to spur romance.

I feigned being Republican—
She said she was a Democrat.
My jaw dropped like a pelican
For acting like a bureaucrat.

She refused to go out with me
And said we had a great divide.
But I was smitten by Jamie
And sought a way to turn the tide.

Her mother ran for governor,
And Jamie worked for her campaign.
Her mother's name was Eleanor—
She owned a regional food chain.

I admired her basic platform
And worked to get her elected.
I touted her proposed reform—
An act they had not expected.

We finally went on a date—
She proved to be a lovely girl.
I thought she'd be a perfect mate
And a bond began to unfurl.

We rarely discussed politics—
It was not a priority.
Our frivolous starting antics
Gave way to love and clarity.

The Politics of Fear

Vile politics has gripped our land,
Based not on substance but on fear.[138]
Politicians don't understand—
Hard work is what the folks revere.

Many are mere obstructionists[139]
Who lack vision and intellect.
They bow to cash from lobbyists
And give the people no respect.[140]

Let's not forget TV pundits
Who shout their version of the truth.
We give these mouthpieces plaudits
When all they do is distort sooth.

Voters must bear some of the blame
For being downright gullible.
Mediocrity is our shame—
It makes deception feasible.[141]

Informed through e-mails, blogs, and tweets,
We dummy up and scholar down.
Smart phones in hand, we roam the streets—
Faking the wisest sage in town.[142]

Let's end the politics of fear—
The country needs civil debate.[143]
Unless we guard what we hold dear,
We risk becoming second rate.

My Way or No Way

Some folks want our leader to fail[144]
Because their party's not in charge.
In a shrewd attempt to prevail
They cheat and bark like a drill sarge.

Such spoilers block the voter's will
By playing demander-in-chief.
They cause Miss Liberty great ill
Just to advance a coaxed belief.[145]

Many of us have no health care,
While others are being foreclosed.
Our troops are engaged in warfare,
And our borders remain exposed.[146]

The Congress is dysfunctional,
And crass ideology reigns.
With government so factional,
Vast despair is all that remains.[147]

My way or no way halts progress,
But all the spoilers should beware.
When they block the nation's success,
They will be caught in their own snare.[148]

My way or no way does wear thin
And does not fix our nation's mess.
All great empires die from within
When government becomes pointless.

The Truth about Opinions

The joy of "getting someone told"
Is just the act of being bold.[149]
It indicates the tongue is loose
And risks silencing by the noose.

We treat opinions as sacred,
Which causes angels to have dread.
We all have one mouth and two ears
To keep us wise throughout our years.

To those who do "lay down the law"—
All it takes is moving the jaw.
Unless you speak the word of God,
Hold tight your tongue or risk the rod.[150]

Opinions are like a great pun—
Each of us has a special one.
They are trite in the scheme of things
And fail to enhance our blessings.[151]

Let's keep opinions to ourselves[152]
And get those good books off our shelves.[153]
Perhaps we'll stop being uncouth
And learn to speak only the truth.[154]

THE COUNTRY

A nation is a community of people occupying a defined territory and united by a single government. Citizens share national pride and a willingness to come to the defense of their beloved nation despite diverse origins or opposing political views. After free and fair elections—as occur in America—opposing sides should be willing to support the leader voted into office by the people. After all it is a government of the people, by the people, for the people, as stated by President Lincoln in his Gettysburg Address.

Lincoln delivered the Gettysburg Address 149 years ago while dedicating a cemetery at the battlefield where the Union won a decisive battle over the Confederacy—a group of eleven states that seceded from the Union over the right to own slaves. While presiding over the Civil War, Lincoln had to contend with venomous oratory from Confederate sympathizers called copperheads—Democrats from states bordering the Confederacy who used states' rights to oppose him.[155]

Today the country is again divided into various factions: blue states/red states, conservatives/liberals, Republicans/Democrats—take your pick.[156] Adherents pledge allegiance to their respective party platforms and not to their country. The economy and health care reform are among the most contentious issues. The president is also opposed by members of his own party who call themselves the Blue Dog Coalition.[157]

Congressional opponents of national health care cite government intrusion into voters' personal lives and the imposition of mandates. Some have resorted to distortions and scare tactics to demonize the president while concealing conflicts of interest resulting from campaign donations received from the insurance industry.[158] Curiously only 3 percent of House Republicans opted out of the Federal Employees Health Benefit Plan.[159] The rate of increase in US health care (HC) costs exceeds the growth of the economy, the rate of inflation, and the rise in wages. In the 2009 rankings of international HC spending, the United States topped the list at 17.6 percent of gross domestic product (Switzerland is in second place at 11.3 percent).[160] Yet America ranks thirty-seventh in HC quality,[161] forty-second in life expectancy,[162] and forty-first in infant mortality.[163] More than half of the $2.2 trillion spent on HC is wasted.[164] The current system is untenable,[165] and single-payer HC,[166] centralized electronic medical records,[167] and tort reform[168] are needed.

Our country is also experiencing a severe economic downturn due in part to unprincipled risk taking by banks and investment firms to increase short-term gains.[169] Profits allow executives to reap obscene bonuses.[170] American companies are also at a disadvantage due to the high cost of HC and labor,[171] restrictions on exports,[172] the devalued Chinese currency,[173] and government subsidies[174] for some foreign industries. A federal bailout of the financial system, initiated by the former administration,[175] was disbursed by the current one. A depression was averted, but the current president has been faulted for bailing out Wall Street and increasing the nation's deficit. He's blamed for not creating jobs as voters buy foreign goods from companies that export US jobs.

Supporting the president is crucial in these troubled times. Stalemate over important issues will not produce solutions— *a nation divided cannot stand*. Fortunately Lincoln prevailed, the Union Army was victorious, and America was kept united. Hopefully we will be delivered from the brink of our current disaster. But for that to happen, voters must inform themselves, avoid being hoodwinked by politicians, and remain united—for *united we stand*.

A Grateful Nation

Our nation sends its troops to war
To lands that are foreign and far.
Deployed without adequate gear[176]
For tours that last beyond a year.

They go and serve with bravery
To keep a wayward nation free.[177]
We keep it quiet when they die
So no one gets to question why.

Troops are robbed of family life,
Which causes them domestic strife.[178]
They risk their lives for such low pay
To guard the American way.

Our nation needs to summon all
Each time it sounds the battle call.[179]
This nation relies on too few
When conflict causes blood to spew.

With endless tours in combat zones,
We treat our precious troops like drones.
And yet the brass cannot decide
Why troops resort to suicide.[180]

They come home with PTSD,[181]
And we accept this tragedy.
It's time for us to reassess
Their mounting cares from combat stress.[182]

We should expand our troop reserves
And give the rest each one deserves.
Recurring tours are inhumane—
They drive both troop and spouse insane.

With excess combat exposure,
We abuse our nation's treasure.[183]
Let's use them to guard our freedom
When faced by a hostile kingdom.

As beacons of world peace and trust
Our causes must be pure and just.
Thus, when faced with tribulation,
God will bless a grateful nation.

Cheap Labor

Americans love cheap labor
To grow the crops we all savor.
Consumers and farmers concur—
We need the "illegal" worker.[184]

Some companies hire coyotes
To smuggle in poor refugees.
They work from morning until night,
And then they must stay out of sight.

When they rise above the radars,
They are cuffed and thrown behind bars.[185]
No one voiced any real concern
Before the financial downturn.

Millions must live in the shadows,[186]
Peering out from behind windows.
Their children fear attending school,
And some forego this basic tool.[187]

They pay social security,[188]
Yet receive insecurity.
Undocumented lack health care,
And we all know this is not fair.

All cheap labor comes at a price
No matter how you slice and dice.
When US companies outsource,
Despair strikes a foreign workforce.[189]

Finding mass labor below cost
Suggests our morals have been tossed.
Poor workers here and overseas
Belong to God's beloved species.

Completely Free

Some want to be completely free
And think it's their God-given right.
But life in a community
Dictates we have broader insight.

In a successful neighborhood,
All members are codependent.
Each person behaves as he should
To be a useful element.

When folks are irresponsible,
They burden the community.
Harmony isn't possibly
When they foil our shared destiny.[190]

When some engage in drug abuse,
Crime increases all around town.
Even excess alcohol use
Will provoke a collective frown.

Don't forget the junk food junkie[191]
Who runs the risk of heart disease.
Not only is his waist chunky
He often gets diabetes.

Some thrive on adrenaline highs
And raise health care costs to the max.[192]
Why should everyone's health costs rise?
They should pay a thrill-seeker's tax.

We all agree life should be fun—
On prudent life we disagree.
Extreme lifestyles cost everyone—
Let's levy a risk-taker's fee.

Our nation values everyone
And has plenty to oversee.
To run amok requires just one
Who acts as if completely free.[193]

Free Enterprise

In the scheme called free enterprise,
Corporations pilfer the prize.
Financial books post a profit
So CEOs can benefit.[194]

They give candidates tons of dough
So they can sway both friend and foe.
Buying favors is now the norm;
That's why they fight campaign reform.

Their schemes fueled a deep recession—
Made some hock their last possession.[195]
When will the voters recognize
The dangers of free enterprise?

Recession dispersed at warp speed
Due mostly to corporate greed.
They got bailed out with aid called TARP;[196]
Bankrupt voters increased like carp.[197]

Politicians allowed the rich
To drive us all into the ditch.
It's time to send the crooks to jail[198]
And not allow them to post bail.

When broke parents are laid to rest,
Kids must pay their debt with interest.[199]
Some folks question democracy
When it condones such lunacy.

We must pass wise regulation
To ease our kids' consternation.
When will the people realize
The need to fix free enterprise?[200]

The Scourge of Drugs

America's use of street drugs
Places our great nation at risk.
Kids die in crossfire caused by thugs[201]
Fighting for drug sales that are brisk.

Drug cartels duel in Mexico
And place entire towns under siege.[202]
From Juárez to Acapulco,
Vile drug kingpins bask in prestige.

Afghans harvest their poppy crop
To finance brutal terrorists.[203]
Crop suppression has been a flop[204]
Because vast corruption persists.[205]

Addiction to Middle East oil
Has left our nation's cupboards bare.
Now drug abuse has seared the soil
Our fathers tilled with loving care.

Our leaders declared a drug war[206]
On the dealer and supplier.
Not even our country's drug czar
Sought to rehab the drug user.[207]

Drug use is not recreation
But a scourge that threatens us all.
It will lead to our destruction
By those who plot to make us fall.

We spend billions to guard our land,[208]
But drug use skirts all protection.
It's time drug users understand
The fallout from their brash action.

They may choose not to self-destruct
If taught the dangers posed by drugs.
Most would end drug-seeking conduct
To bankrupt vile drug-pushing slugs.

It's time to come to our senses
Or compose our funeral dirge.
We can shore up our defenses
By ending the drug abuse scourge.

Popular News

Popular news fills the airwaves
With what the average Joe craves.
It comes in thirty-second bites
Followed by pundits' verbal fights.

They fill Joe's mind with conjured "facts"
Then wait to see how he reacts.
The host pulls Joe into the fray
Through blogs and tweets to have his say.[209]

In our hooked-up digital age,
Average Joe takes the world stage.
Broadcasting him through his webcam
Is not good news—it's just a sham.

Bureaus prefer their cheap pop news;[210]
They're not required to pay their dues.
With no who, what, when, why, and where,
Journalism has been stripped bare.

Short on substance, long on ratings,[211]
The news is made with great savings.
It's news networks can expedite
Without the finesse of Cronkite.

Some news is an infomercial
Given by a bribed official.
There should be ample disclosure
Of slick campaign-fund indenture.

A well-informed electorate
Would have bureaus corroborate.
They'd insist on substantive news
And far less of glib pundits' views.

The news should serve to enlighten—
A fact bureaus have forgotten.[212]
Pop news is a euphemism
For substandard journalism.

Control through Adjudication

The nation has come to crossroads
In the fight to control power.
As major voting blocs erode,[213]
We approach a crucial hour.

Our land will have an ethnic shift[214]
Where whites are the minority,
So courts ruled the corporate gift
Should have supreme authority.[215]

It all began with *Gore v. Bush*[216]
Where courts trumped the popular vote.
The Congress ignored the ambush—
Thus partial judges rule and gloat.

Once more the court has overreached
By enabling corporations.
The people's control has been breached
Through judicial litigations.[217]

Activist judges have sold out[218]
To powerful corporations.
Because they threw a crucial bout,
Campaign gifts control elections.

If Congress does not legislate,
We may lose our democracy.
They must let folks control their fate
And reject oligocracy.[219]

Courts disregard our melting pot—
The backbone of this great country.
Without firing a single shot
They raze the laws that keep us free.

By taking voters to the mat,
The Supreme Court snubbed the nation.
The Congress must halt attempts at
Control through adjudication.

The Unemployment Blame Game

Americans play the blame game
With the high unemployment rate.[220]
The farce is a terrible shame
When how we spend controls our fate.

We should reject cheap foreign goods
From those who don't buy much from us.
Products made in our neighborhoods
Could even spark a job surplus.

Domestic cars would help save jobs,
But we keep buying Japanese.
Such mindless spending makes us snobs
And brings the country to its knees.

Companies send jobs overseas
To avoid workers' benefits,
Yet we rebuff Obama's pleas
To end tax breaks for these misfits.[221]

Some say he mars free enterprise—
The same ones who buy foreign goods.
When will the people realize
They are snubbing their neighborhoods.

Some companies choose to outsource
To circumvent regulations.[222]
They bring kids into the workforce[223]
Through foreign conglomerations.

Lead-tainted toys[224] and putrid fish[225]
Make for never-ending recalls.
While shameless exporters flourish,
The idle worker's lifestyle falls.

Foreigners bootleg our products
And perfect reverse production.[226]
Our economy deconstructs
As we buy cheap reproductions.

We put our people out of work
When we buy goods made overseas.
The jobless rate drives us berserk
But greatly profits the Chinese.

Let's state the source of each product
As a basic consumer right.[227]
Exporters wrought with misconduct—
Consumers can boycott outright.

Trade deficits hurt like hammers[228]
Swung by trade "partners" with contempt.[229]
Yet the world's foremost consumers
Can't muster a counter-attempt.

We shirk responsibility;
Yet, reject American wares.
Since we share culpability,
Let's bond to solve our jobless cares.

Our national security
Leans on our economic strength.
Make slack buying a rarity
And check origin at great length.

We must rally true patriots
To guard both mom and apple pie.
Then tell all slack compatriots,
"Shop wise and let the blame game die."

Government Exploitation

Faithful government employees
Are treated like loathsome payees.[230]
They want to make us less than slaves
To prevent us from making waves.

Once robbed of our bargaining rights,
We're forced to work weekends and nights.
Many of us don't use our leave
For fear of engendering peeve.

The boss fills the workplace with stress
And makes workers do more with less.
Productivity has increased
Since workers' rights have all but ceased.

The middle class is under siege[231]
While rich folks gain wealth and prestige.
Both public and private workers
Grow weary as their hope flickers.

Some workers vote for demagogues
Who recite scripted monologues.[232]
When will beleaguered workers learn
They invite political spurn?

The middle class forms the tax base
That Congressmen splurge and erase.
Tax relief goes to those with wealth;[233]
Others reap poor financial health.

We pay social security,
That wanes with our maturity.
Congress "borrows" some of the fund;[234]
But, their pensions remain rotund.

Government loathes the middle class
And caters to the upper class.
They always scratch each other's back
And let workers fall through the crack.

Our states attack bargaining rights
And take retirement from our sights.
They'll always dictate our choices
Until we unite our voices.

The President's Critics

The president's critics grumble,
Hoping to make POTUS tumble.
Most hail from the gridlocked Congress—
A group skilled at foiling progress.

Congress fought *Forty-Four* for spite
And furthered our declining might.
They fail to do the people's work,
But grasped onto each unearned perk.

Both parties keep their feuding brisk
And place the nation at great risk.[235]
Then they urge each husband and spouse
To vote them into the White House.

Some don't deserve the time of day,
Yet many folks send votes their way.
They serve us with ineptitude—
The POTUS should have aptitude.

Some congressmen are impotent
And fan the flames of discontent.
They'd rather toe the party line[236]
Than right our nation's slow decline.

Candidates run for president
By deceiving each resident.
They squelch our power in numbers
By misleading he who slumbers.[237]

Beware of those who want to rob
The nation when they get the job.
Many of them are so lacking
They deserve a good shellacking.

Should the nation run out of steam,
Her people will no longer dream.[238]
The uninformed constituent
Will succumb to the affluent.

Rid Congress of blood-sucking ticks
Thru wisely studied politics.
America's best patriots
Are well-informed compatriots.

ECONOMY

A nation's economy refers to how the country manages its income and expenditures through the use of its resources to create wealth to sustain its people. Wealth distribution should be equitable—especially in a democracy. In contrast, an autocracy (dictatorship), aristocracy (rule by a privileged few), or banana republic (plutocracy or oligarchy) distributes much of its wealth to one person or a select few.

America's wealth emanates from its people (the source of labor and innovation) and natural resources (the land). The land destined to become America was already occupied by several million Indians when European settlers invaded its shores. Their arrival proved disastrous for the Indians. The diseases transported from Europe, against which the Indians had no immunity, had calamitous consequences. The natives were also decimated by gun-bearing European visitors who invoked divine providence (manifest destiny) to justify taking land from the non-Christian aboriginal inhabitants.

Christopher Columbus arrived in 1492. The English established their first permanent settlement at Jamestown, Virginia, in 1602 with assistance from the Powhatan Indians. The New World economy was initiated by utilizing laborers from Europe—since most native inhabitants resisted servitude. More than two-thirds of English immigrants came to the colonies as indentured servants,[239] agreeing to work three-to-seven years in exchange for the cost of passage to the New World. As many as half died before completing their obligation. Some Europeans chose servitude in the colonies as an alternative to serving prison terms for crimes committed at home.

After their arrival many indentured servants were trained as skilled laborers in a variety of trades. Upon completion of their servitude, they were freed; some went into business for themselves, plying their newly acquired trades. Others rejected manufacturing, settled on tracts of land, and went into farming. This caused a shortage of skilled laborers and raised labor costs.

Colonial governments vigorously protected the financial interests of the masters and employers and showed less concern for the rights of indentured servants or freedmen. They held firm to the notion that every able-bodied man should work. Settlers who committed minor offenses were sometimes sentenced to work on public projects. Officials in some locales passed regulations that placed a ceiling on wages and assigned a minimum number of work hours due to the labor shortages.[240]

The labor system for African slaves was inhumane. It began two centuries before the settlement of Virginia and provided stable labor for plantation owners who grew tobacco, rice, and indigo. Once purchased, slaves provided a lifetime of uncompensated labor that formed the economic system of the Deep South.[241] Codes made slaves inheritable property, restricted their movement, and enacted a harsh system of discipline.

By 1775 there were a half-million blacks in the country, and more than three-fifths lived in Virginia and South Carolina. Sullivan Island, South Carolina, was the Ellis Island for slavery,[242] and Africans constituted the majority of that state's population. The invention of the cotton gin in 1793 made cotton very profitable and cotton became "king" in the South. Cotton growers with considerable acreage and many slaves became very wealthy.

During the American Revolution, freed white males improved their social status by enlisting in the Continental Army or state militia. Some indentured servants enlisted in the Patriot army in exchange for release from their servitude, which drew protests from their masters. After the revolution servitude continued to flourish but finally ended for whites during the Jackson administration. Slavery continued for blacks and the attitude of Southern slave owners toward their "property" hardened. A civil war was required to free the slaves.

Ridding the land of its indigenous people and ignoring workers' rights were paramount in establishing the nation's economy. Workers had to organize and utilize the much-maligned strike to establish rights for themselves. Today several states resort to the abolishment of collective bargaining to reduce budgetary short-falls.[243] Private employers trim labor costs by paying less than living wages, reducing health care benefits, and cutting retirement packages. Other cost-cutting tactics include outsourcing,[244] moving to right-to-work states,[245] and moving production facilities out of the country.

President Clinton signed NAFTA[246] into law in 1993, and it—along with lopsided trade between the United States and Asian countries[247]—has adversely affected US jobs and the economy. Manufacturing—the economic incubator for the middle class—has been devastated since idle workers were unprepared to shift to other occupations that require vastly different skills.

Currently 60 percent of all we buy is made overseas,[248] including 100 percent of iPods[249] and more than 70 percent of items sold in Walmart stores.[250] Yet Congress continues to insist on unbridled "free trade," refuses to regulate financial institutions, and won't repeal tax breaks for those who divert American jobs to overseas sweatshops. Instead they coddle corporations and the rich to finance their continuous campaigns. Ironically consumers fault the president for not creating jobs as they continue to buy cheap products made by exploited foreign workers.

The cozy relationship between corporations and politicians was strengthen by a recent Supreme Court ruling stating that corporate and union campaign contributions are a form of free speech, effectively striking down limits placed on contributions during federal elections.[251] The ruling will forever change the face of democracy in America.

While stumping in Iowa, Mitt Romney stated that corporations are people.[252] The relationship between politicians and large donors is a clear and present danger. Congress and the courts have aided corporate rights at the expense of individual voter rights.

Social security is funded by payroll taxes taken from working people. The social security trust fund is backed by the "full faith and credit of the federal government." Yet when Congress came perilously close to not raising the debt ceiling and causing the United States to default, the president acknowledged that social security recipients might not get paid.[253] This confirmed that the social security trust fund has no *real* assets. The $2.6 trillion it was alleged to have is gone.[254] Thus retired social security recipients are at the mercy of Congress.

The great recession of 2008 was due in large part to unsavory practices by financial institutions. Millions of American homes have been foreclosed and 22 percent of all US home mortgages are underwater.[255] Americans continue to lose jobs to countries that have blatant disregard for workers' rights, have little concern for safety, and allow goods to be manufactured under sweatshop conditions.[256]

Congress can now receive unlimited campaign contributions from the corporations and financial institutions it is tasked with overseeing. This conflict of interest is a problem of immense proportion; it threatens to make a mockery of our democracy and the free enterprise system.

Voter apathy—and an overreliance on politicians and slanted news media[257] for education on political and economic matters—has contributed to America's decline. Meanwhile pressing problems such as rising health care costs, the national debt, trade deficits, tax reform, campaign financing reform, burgeoning entitlement programs, shoddy public education, porous borders, immigration reform, wealth distribution inequities, middle-class contraction, decaying infrastructure, and the mortgage crisis are simply deferred to the next generation.

After troubled financial institutions received voter-funded bailouts through TARP, banks refused to work with homeowners whose mortgages were underwater. Mitt Romney's solution is to allow the process to run its course so investors can purchase the properties and rent them out.[258] It's time for voters to weigh in on this and other important problems facing our nation.[259]

The term *Arab Spring* describes the prodemocracy uprising that swept the Middle East and North Africa in the spring of 2011.

Inequities in wealth distribution, government corruption, high unemployment, and human rights violations were to blame.[260]

Economic inequities, joblessness, and Congress' pandering to corporations increase the likelihood of a "rebirth" of democracy in America. The top 1 percent of citizens own 43 percent of the wealth, while the lower 80 percent own only 7 percent. Corporate tax revenues as a percentage of GDP are nearing historic lows.[261] Corporations stockpile cash at record rates,[262] resist hiring, export jobs to foreign workers, and have undue influence on the election of public officials. General Electric paid no taxes in 2010 after making $5.1 billion and also claimed a $3.2 billion tax credit.[263] Some corporations avoid paying taxes altogether by moving their headquarters offshore.[264]

Democracy denotes rule by the people—not by aristocrats, corporations, or lobbyists. Congress refuses to address the trade imbalance, housing crisis, unemployment rate,[265] collapse of the middle class,[266] dramatic rise in poverty[267] and hunger[268] in America, and influx of foreign products (despite exorbitant trade deficits). Instead Congress abides the obscene wealth enjoyed by a few and remains gridlocked, while economic woes threaten the security of our nation. Many Republicans have signed a pledge with conservative lobbyist Grover Norquist to not raise taxes.[269]

Meanwhile China has become the biggest exporter in the global economy,[270] aided by its devalued currency.[271] China is the largest trading partner of Africa,[272] ASEAN,[273] Brazil,[274] EU,[275] Iran,[276] Japan,[277] Peru,[278] Russia,[279] and others.

Our corrupt government officials are incapable of managing America's income and expenditures and are negligent in utilizing resources wisely. Since they lack the decency to resign, we the people should abandon our allegiance to both political parties. We can begin anew by electing officials who will pledge to mend public education, balance the budget, regulate free enterprise, simplify the tax code, conserve resources, put Americans back to work, improve our standing in the global economy, protect the environment, and avoid gridlock in government.

Democracy is not guaranteed. It requires a collective purpose, careful oversight, informed voters, secure borders, astute leadership, love for one another, and trust in God.

> America will never be destroyed from the outside. If we falter and lose our freedoms, it will be because we destroyed ourselves.
> —Abraham Lincoln

Let Economic Freedom Ring

America the beautiful
Has become much less bountiful.
We ravaged the economy
And mortgaged our autonomy.[280]

We've lost our top credit rating[281]
And keep our creditors waiting.
Yet, Washington won't slow spending—
Knowing bankruptcy is pending.

The Congress botched the debt ceiling
And made themselves less appealing.
Both parties tout their own gadget—
Neither balances the budget.[282]

For the voter it's implicit—
Congress must cut the deficit.
But they choose to remain gridlocked;
Their insolence has left folks shocked.

We should give Congress an order
To make spending cuts much broader.
They cater to special interests
And make the voters their footrests.

Due to failing infrastructure,
We fear old gas lines will rupture.[283]
Before crossing a bridge, we pray,[284]
"Lord, let us see another day."

Japanese fly on bullet trains,[285]
While we get grounded on airplanes.[286]
The need for mass transit is high,
But Congress skimps this piece of pie.[287]

The power grid crawls like rush hour
And can't cope with spikes in power.[288]
Some cars run on charged batteries,
Which adds to growing grid worries.

Our nation's wealth is shared by few,
And the poor are rendered obscure.
The middle class is shrinking fast,
But tax loopholes remain steadfast.

Executives bask in Belize
While voters' jobs go overseas.
There soon will be just rich and poor;
The middle class will be no more.

Reagan said wealth would trickle down—
But, his view was just a shakedown.
Congress supports corporate greed
So they can get more campaign seed.

Congress retains the Bush tax breaks—
A rich man keeps all that he makes.
Most voters lack financial health,
Because a few hoard all the wealth.

We send our brave troops off to war
And bring them home with stress and mar.[289]
They fight and leave our foes destroyed—
Once home they join the unemployed.[290]

Most new jobs that are created
Pay less than anticipated.[291]
We no longer manufacture
But work in travel and leisure.

Some folks tout globalization,
But it seems to harm our nation.[292]
The trade deficit skyrockets,
While the Congress touts free markets.

Politicians are unbending,
And their discord is unending.
The greatest nation on the earth
Is in dire need of a rebirth.

Let economic freedom ring,
Or risk an American Spring.
Let's halt the aristocracy
And build a true democracy.

Capitol Hill Kids at Play

Republicans spawned kids who say—
"Vote my way or hit the highway."
Such kids will never compromise,
So gridlock comes as no surprise.

Some of them formed a Tea Party;
It made them feel grown and haughty.
They snubbed the adults on the Hill
To exercise their childish will.

Kids should never touch the purse strings[293]
Or deal with other crucial things.
They need serious informing
On facts such as global warming.[294]

They push fossil fuel energy[295]
That disrupts nature's synergy.
Even after the Gulf oil spill,
It did not faze kids on the Hill.

Kids love cheap stuff made in China—
That kills jobs in Carolina.
Since it profits corporations,
They ignore voter frustrations.

Kids rant for jobs and free markets—
So firms can deepen their pockets.
They turn to cheap offshore sources
To cut their human resources.

As more jobs go across the sea,
The kids can't see the lunacy.
Low taxes are kids holy grail;
Their tax pledge was too grand to fail.

Kids at play hate regulation,[296]
Which stirs voter consternation.
Following a harsh recession,
They oppose a wise concession.

The kids toyed with the debt ceiling[297]
And sent global markets reeling.
They ignore the trade deficit;
Their deeds bordered on illicit.

They idolize Reaganomics—
Plain ole voodoo economics.[298]
The wealth will never trickle down;[299]
Rich folks stockpile their spoils uptown.

Kids say jobs surge with low taxes,[300]
And so the unemployed waxes.
The Bush tax cuts brought few new jobs;
Bill's tax hikes employed idled mobs.

Claims of federal intrusion
Suggests they are in collusion.
Kids know folks don't trust government
To reap and share the nation's mint.

They malign federal power;
But, what makes the voters cower
Are Texans who want to secede[301]
To provoke a southern stampede.

We need to remind the Lone Star—
The Union won the Civil War.
Though brash kids can be divisive,
Reprimand can be decisive.

Hill kids dashed out for their recess,
And left their House in quite a mess.[302]
During the break they gathered dough
To stage another campaign show.

They sought to make Obama fail[303]
By making voters writhe and wail.
Kids sought to grab the nations reigns—
By ramping up our fiscal pains.

Kids need adult supervision;
Yet, oppose it with derision.
They slurred the White House resident—
To elect a vile president.

The Hill is not a place for kids—
They'll put the nation on the skids.
Kids sneeze and make the nation ill—
They must be banished from the Hill.

Knowledge Is Power

Well-trained workers drive fiscal growth
And ensure a first-rate workforce.
Our economy can't go forth
Unless our schools get back on course.

Local school financing must change;[304]
It leaves strapped counties with poor schools.[305]
The current method seems so strange
For funding the wisest of tools.[306]

When public schools don't make the grade,
Our students fail to measure up.
As dreams and hopes begin to fade,
Some kids are destined for lockup.[307]

We should educate every child;
So, why has Congress cut Head Start?
They wonder why voters get riled
When they refuse to do their part.

Early Head Start helps deprived kids
Make progress in school as they should.[308]
Mugging these poor kids—God forbids—
Shows Congress acts like "Robbing" Hood.

Asian economic strength soars
With high scores in math and science.[309]
We buy their cheap stuff sent to stores
From sweatshops with a clear conscience.

While many public schools stagnate,
Congress search for a solution.
Then the chose to eliminate—
Department of Education.[310]

The Congress needs educating—
The trade deficit trumps their math.
With our exports decimating,
They seem stunned by the aftermath.

Schools profit us at every stage
And keep us more competitive.
Our nation's decline as world sage
Proves schools should be more substantive.

We give our teachers disrespect
With resources that shrink their worth.
The nation has said in effect,
It abides our kids' mental dearth.

We endow our cell phones with smarts
But leave our children's minds to waste.[311]
It's time we mend our shameful hearts
And fix our shoddy schools with haste.

We need to design smart classes—
Managed by certified teachers.[312]
Then instruct our lads and lasses
Through multimedia features.

States could set their curriculum
With corresponding lesson plans.
Student achievement would be plum
With fewer trite teacher demands.

Lectures filled with animations
Would be both exciting and thrift.
Paired with classroom demonstrations,
It would be a paradigm shift.

States could devise and grade kids' tests—
Accomplished through the internet.
Teachers could meet other requests
To assure their state's goals are met.

All of us need to value school
And choose leaders who feel the same.
The status quo is just not cool
As Asia puts us all to shame.

In the quest for fiscal power
We can't allow kids' minds to waste.
Put to the test, they will cower
Unless schools are stellar and chaste.

For us to remain strong and free,
We must lead the quest for knowledge.
Competent schools will be the key
That keeps us on the leading edge.

To Whom Much Is Given, Much Is Expected

The world's greatest economy
Has flourished from autonomy.
We never had to bend our knees
To a string of harsh enemies.

Our land stretches from sea to sea,
And both of our neighbors are free.
Resources are varied and vast,
But we must plan to make them last.

We flex our military might
As though we really love to fight.
Many people who live afar,
Are left to think we relish war.

Some say we are the world's police
Because we try to keep the peace.
Better use of diplomacy
Might build a better legacy.

Many nations are wrought with woes
From corrupt leaders or by foes.
Most of our woes come from within,
From politics that's wearing thin.

We are rich or poor, red or blue,
In a land God blessed through and through.
The world's foremost economy
Has become a dichotomy.

Sometimes we spread ourselves too thin;
It ramps up pressure from within.
We disagree and wring our hands—
While drought and strife fill other lands.

The world's too big to guard alone,
And yet the UN has not shone.
Coming together is a must
To prove it is In God We Trust.

Our nation has been given much—
We flourish from God's blessed touch.
Because so much is expected,
Let's praise God and get connected.

Notes

1 Newton, Barry. "A Short Handbook on Love." *SJChurchofChrist*. 2002. Accessed November 1, 2011, http://www.sjchurchofchrist. org/websitepublisher/a-short-handbook-on-love.html
2 1 Corinthians 13:4–8.
3 "Marriage Love: Agapé." *ChristianMatrimony*. Accessed November 1, 2011, http://www.christian-matrimony.com/ marriag_love_agape.php
4 John 15:12–13.
5 Hebrews 11:1–40.
6 Szulc, Tad. "Abraham: Journey of Faith." *National Geographic*. Accessed Oct. 29, 2011, http://ngm.nationalgeographic.com/ ngm/data/2001/12/01/html/ft_20011201.6.html
7 Romans 4:1–25.
8 Luke 16:13–14.
9 Barker, Kenneth, ed. *The NIV Study Bible*, 10th ed. Grand Rapids: Zondervan, 1995.
10 "Western Wall, Jerusalem." *Sacred Destination*. Updated, November 20, 2009, http://www.sacred-destinations.com/ israel/jerusalem-western-wall
11 Ezra 1:1–7.
12 "Surat Al-Isra' (Night Journey)." *Qur'an*. Accessed November 1, 2011, http://quran.com/17
13 Bauer, Brent A. "Can Yucca Relieve Pain?" *MayoClinic*. June 28, 2011, http://www.mayoclinic.com/health/arthritis/ AN01107
14 "Church of the Holy Sepulchre, Jerusalem." *Sacred Destinations*. Last updated Feb. 21, 2010, http://www.sacred-destinations.com/israel/jerusalem-church-of-holy-sepulchre
15 Zechariah 14:16–19.
16 Psalm: 147: 12–14.
17 John 1:1–3.
18 Matthew 4: 4.
19 Acts 2:1–4.

20 2 Corinthians 4:7–9.

21 John 14:1–2.

22 2 Corinthians 9:6.

23 Genesis 1:26.

24 Revelation 1:7.

25 2 Chronicles 6:5–6.

26 Psalm 76: 1–12.

27 Isa 64:8.

28 Bryant-Work, Linda. "Students Writing Skills Diminished by Text Messaging." *PlainsPress*. March 7, 2010, http://www.southplainscollege.edu/ppress/issue_09_11/feature/student_feature_09_11.htm

29 Romans 5:1–5.

30 2 Corinthians 5:10.

31 2 Corinthians 5:7.

32 Gronewold, Nathanial. "Africa Drought Endangers Millions." *NYTimes*. July 5, 2011, http://www.nytimes.com/cwire/2011/07/05/05climatewire-africa-drought-endangers-millions-22493.html?pagewanted=print

33 Romm, Joe. "USGS Exert Explains How Global Warming Likely Contributes to East Africa's Brutal Drought." *ThinkProgress*. October 19, 2011, http://thinkprogress.org/romm/2011/10/19/348335/usgs-expert-explains-how-global-warming-likely-contributes-to-east-africas-brutal-drought/#

34 Thomas, G. Scott. "America's 10 Most Affluent Communities." *BizJournal*. September 16, 2011, http://www.bizjournals.com/bizjournals/on-numbers/scott-thomas/2011/09/americas-10-most-affluent-communities.html?s=print

35 Revelations 3:17.

36 Berger, Brian. "NASA to Unveil Plans to Send 4 Astronauts to the Moon in 2018." *Space*. September 14, 2011, http://www.space.com/1553-nasa-unveil-plans-send-4-astronauts-moon-2018.html

37 Genesis 3:19.

38 Matthew 6:1.

39 Mathew 6:3.

40 "Top Rated Charities." *Charity Watch*. Accessed October 30, 2011, http://www.charitywatch.org/toprated.html

41 Jonah 1:1–2.

42 Jonah 4:10–11.

43 1 Corinthians 13:13.

44 Jonah 1:3.

45 Jonah 2:8.

46 Jonah 2:9–10.

47 "Sudan - Darfur Overview." *UNICEF*. October 2008, accessed November 28, 2011, http://www.unicef.org/infobycountry/ sudan_darfuroverview.html

48 "Sudanese Leader Still Committing Crimes in Darfur, Security Council Told." *UN*. June 8, 2011, http://www.un.org/apps/ news/story.asp?NewsID=38660&Cr=darfur&Cr1

49 Revelation 3:15–17.

50 Proverbs 28:12.

51 "The Republican Party is the Pro-life Party." *RNCL*. updated 2001, accessed November 14, 2011, http://www.rnclife.org/ brochure/rprolife.html

52 "Uninsured Children." *Children Defense Fund*. Accessed November 1, 2011, http://www.childrensdefense.org/policy-priorities/childrens-health/uninsured-children/

53 "U.S. Infant Mortality Rate Worse Than in Forty Other Countries." *IBTimes*. August 31, 2011 1:41 PM EDT, http://www.ibtimes.com/ articles/206614/20110831/u-s-infant-mortality-infant-mortality-u-s-infant-mortality-america-infant-mortality-rates.htm

54 Jacobson, Jodi. "GOP Loves Government-Sponsored Health Care...For Themselves." *RHRealityCheck*. January 19, 2011, http://www.rhrealitycheck.org/blog/2011/01/19/loves-governmentsponsored-health-carefor-themselves

55 "UNICEF and WHO Launch Report on Diarrhea, the Second Greatest Killer of Children." *UNICEFUSA*. October 14, 2009, http://www.unicefusa.org/news/releases/unicef-and-who-launch-report.html

56 Tarler, Thomas. "Denver Is Ignoring the Homeless Citizens." *DUClarion*. October 30, 2011, http://www.duclarion.com/opinions/denver-is-ignoring-the-homeless-citizens-1.2674293

57 Matthew 25:34–40.

58 Grant, Kelli B. "The Important Charities You're Ignoring." SmartMoney. June 20, 2011, http://blogs.smart-money.com/paydirt/2011/06/20/the-important-charities-you%E2%80%99re-ignoring/

59 Matthew 25:43–46.

60 Tampkins, Theresa. "Medical Bills Prompt More that 60% of Bankruptcies." *CNNHealth*. June 5, 2009, http://articles.cnn.com/2009-06-05/health/bankruptcy.medical.bills_1_medical-bills-bankruptcies-health-insurance?_s=PM:HEALTH

61 Ross, Janell. "U.S. Cities Criminalize Homelessness, Violate Human Rights Agreement". *HuffPost*. August 26, 2011, http://www.huffingtonpost.com/2011/08/26/us-cities-criminalize-homeless_n_938095.html

62 Pelley, Scott. "Homeless Children: The Hard Times Generation." *CBSNews*. Updated June 20, 2011, http://www.cbsnews.com/stories/2011/06/26/60minutes/main20072626.shtml

63 "Human Rights, Homelessness and Health Care." *NHCHC*. Accessed November 14, 2011http://www.nhchc.org/human-right.html

64 Luke 10:29–37.

65 James 2:14.

66 Luke:10:25–28.

67 Censky, Annalyn. "Poverty Rate Rises in America." *CNNMoney*. September 13, 2011, http://money.cnn.com/2011/09/13/news/economy/poverty_rate_income/index.htm

68 Soronen, Rita. "Overseas Babies Displace U.S. Orphans." *BusinessWeek*. February 2008, accessed February 28, 2011, http://www.businessweek.com/debateroom/archives/2008/02/overseas_babies_displace_us_orphans.html

69 James 1:27.

70 "A Lesson From Loughner." *NationalReview*. January 13, 2011, http://www.nationalreview.com/articles/257058/lesson-loughner-editors

71 Lederer, Edith M. "Widows in Poverty: Over 115 Million Widows Live In Devastating Poverty." *HuffPost*. June 23, 2010, http://www.huffingtonpost.com/2010/06/23/widows-in-poverty_n_622110.html

72 "Facts About Rain Forests." *Nature*. Accessed November 14, 2011. http://www.nature.org/ourinitiatives/urgentissues/rain-forests/rainforests-facts.xml

73 Adam, David. "Amazon Could Shrink by 85% Due to Climate Change, Scientists Say." *Guardian*. March 11, 2009, http://www.guardian.co.uk/environment/2009/mar/11/amazon-global-warming-trees/print

74 "Measuring the Daily Destruction of World's Rain Forest." *Scientific American*. November 19,2009, http://www.scientificamerican.com/article.cfm?id=earth-talks-daily-destruction

75 Farabee, M. J. "Photosynthesis" *EMC.Maricopa.edu*. Modified May 18, 2010, accessed November 28, 2011, http://www.emc.maricopa.edu/faculty/farabee/biobk/biobookps.html

76 "Carbon Cycle." Living Rain Forest. Accessed November 14, 2011. http://www.livingrainforest.org/charity/ec-integrated-greenhouse-project/extra-information/carbon-cycle/

77 "What Is Acid Rain?" *EPA*. Updated June 8, 2007, http://www.epa.gov/acidrain/what/index.html

78 "Mercury: Basic Information." *EPA*. Accessed November 15, 2011, http://www.epa.gov/hg/about.htm

79 "Mercury Contamination in Fish." *NRDC*. Accessed November 15, 2011, http://www.nrdc.org/health/effects/mercury/effects.asp

80 Danson, Ted. "Fishing Weaponry." *Oceana: Our Endangered Oceans and What We Can Do to Save Them* (New York: Rodale, 2011), 130–133.

81 "Threat 2: Predator Loss." *SaveOurSeas*. Accessed November 15, 2001, http://saveourseas.com/threats/predatorloss

82 "The Milky Way Galaxy." *UCSD*. Accessed November 15, 2011, http://casswww.ucsd.edu/archive/public/tutorial/MW.html

83 "Recent Warming of Artic May Affect Worldwide Climate." *NASA*. October 23, 2003, http://www.nasa.gov/centers/goddard/news/topstory/2003/1023esuice.html

84 Stöckli, Reto. "Blue Marble." *NASA*. February 8, 2002, accessed November 15, 2011, http://visibleearth.nasa.gov/view_rec.php?id=2429

85 Vermaas, Wim. "Photosynthesis." *ASU*. June 12, 2007, http://bioenergy.asu.edu/photosyn/education/photointro.html

86 "Global Warming Puts Artic On Thin Ice." *NRDC*. Revised November 22, 2005, http://www.nrdc.org/globalwarming/qthinice.asp

87 "Deforestation." *NationalGeographic*. Accessed November 15, 2011, http://environment.nationalgeographic.com/environment/global-warming/deforestation-overview/

88 Weier, John. "Bright Lights, Big City." *NASA*. October 19, 2000, http://earthobservatory.nasa.gov/Features/Lights/

89 "Global Warming." *NYTimes*. Updated September 12, 2011, http://topics.nytimes.com/top/news/science/topics/global-warming/index.html#

90 Mencimer, Stephenie. "Bumper Mentality." *Washington Monthly*. December 2002, http://www.washingtonmonthly.com/features/2001/0212.mencimer.html

91 Kiley, David. "What We Already Knew: TV Ads Are Less Effective. But Then Again, It Depends On Who's Making Them." *BloombergBusinessWeek*. March 22, 2006, http://www.businessweek.com/the_thread/brandnewday/archives/2006/03/what_we_already.html

92 "Twenty Things You Can Do To Conserve Energy." *PowerScoreCard*. Accessed November 15, 2011, http://www.powerscorecard.org/reduce_energy.cfm

93 "California Farm Land at Risk in Budget Battle." *WesternFarmPress*. May 4, 2011, http://westernfarmpress.com/markets/california-farmland-risk-budget-battle

94 "Global Warming Causes Severe Storms." *ScienceDaily*. January 1, 2009, http://www.sciencedaily.com/videos/2009/0109-global_warming_causes_severe_storms.htm

95 Saad, Lydia. "Increased Number Think Global Warming Is 'Exaggerated'." *Gallup*. March 11, 2009, http://www.gallup.com/poll/116590/increased-number-think-global-warming-exaggerated.aspx

96 Dowdy, Sarah. "What Is Clean Coal Technology?" *HowStuffworks*. Accessed November 15, 2011, http://science.howstuffworks.com/environmental/green-science/clean-coal.htm

97 Conniff, Richard. "The Myth of Clean Coal." *YaleEnviron360*. June 3, 2008, http://e360.yale.edu/feature/the_myth_of_clean_coal/2014/

98 "Mercury and Air Toxics Standards (MATS)." *EPA*. October 21, 2011, http://www.epa.gov/airquality/powerplanttoxics/index.html

99 Walsh, Bryan. "Exposing the Myth of Clean Coal." *Time-Science*. January 10,2009, http://www.time.com/time/health/article/0,8599,1870599,00.html

100 McCardle, John. "Michigan Lawmaker Decries 'Clean Coal' Technology, W, Va. Industry." *NYTimes*. August 24, 2011, http://www.nytimes.com/gwire/2011/08/24/24greenwire-michigan-lawmaker-decries-clean-coal-technolog-76443.html

101 "Gasification Technology R&D." *U.S.DOE*. Accessed November 15, 2011, http://www.fossil.energy.gov/programs/ powersystems/gasification/index.html

102 Faila, Nathan. "How Meat Contributes to Global Warming [preview]." *ScientificAmerican*. February 4, 2009, http://www.scientificamerican.com/article.cfm?id=the-greenhouse-hamburger

103 "U.S. Beef and Cattle Industry: Background Statistics and Information." *USDA*. Updated May 25, 2011, http://www.ers.usda.gov/news/BSECoverage.htm

104 "Livestock a Major Threat to Environment." *FAO*. November 29, 2006, http://www.fao.org/newsroom/en/news/2006/1000448/index.html

105 "Pollution on the Hoof." *LA Times*. October 15, 2007, http://articles.latimes.com/2007/oct/15/opinion/ed-methane15

106 "Carbon Footprint Calculator." *CarbonFootprint*. Accessed November 15, 2011, http://www.carbonfootprint.com/calculator.aspx

107 Moyer, Michael. "The Dirty Truth about Plug-In Hybrids." *Scientific American*. Vol. 303, no. 1 (2010): 54–55.

108 Mitchell, Russ. "World Population Will Reach 7 Billion." *CBSNews*. October 29, 2011, http://www.cbsnews.com/8301-18563_162-20127508/world-population-will-reach-7-billion/

109 "Environmental Impacts From Unsustainable Population Growth." *Overpopulation.org*. November 11, 2011, http://www.overpopulation.org/impact.html

110 Bassett, Laura. "Free Birth Control Religious Exemption Coverage Sparks Controversy." *HuffPost*. November 15, 2011, http://www.huffingtonpost.com/2011/08/01/free-birth-control-religious-exemption_n_915381.html?view=screen

111 Fletcher, Sam. "Market Watch: Crude oil prices increase, Challenges $100/bbl in NY Market." *OGJ*. November 14, 2011, http://www.ogj.com/articles/2011/11/market-watch-crude-oil-prices-increase-challenge-100-bbl-in-ny-market.html

112 "Arctic National Wildlife Refuge, 1003 Area, Petroleum Assessment, 1998, Including Economic Analysis." *USGS*. Revised December 4, 2008, http://pubs.usgs.gov/fs/fs-0028-01/fs-0028-01.htm

113 Beinecke, Frances. "America Is Not Prepared to Safely Drill ANWAR." *USNews*. November 3, 2011, http://www.usnews.com/debate-club/is-it-time-to-drill-in-the-arctic-refuge/america-is-not-prepared-to-safely-drill-in-anwr

114 "Potential Impact of Proposed Oil and Gas Development on the Arctic Refuge's Coastal Plain: Historic Overview and

Issues of Concern." *FWS*. February 26, 2009, http://arctic.fws.gov/issues1.htm#section4

115 Sherwonit, Bill. "Arctic Tundra Is Being Lost As Far North Quickly Warms." *YaleEnviron360*. January 11, 2010, http://e360.yale.edu/content/feature.msp?id=2229

116 Arendt, Anthony. "Assessing the Status of Alaska's Glaciers." *ScienceMag*. May 27, 2011, http://www.sciencemag.org/content/332/6033/1044.summary

117 Sheehan, Genevieve. "Tuvalu Little, Tuvalu Late: A Country Goes Under." *Harvard Intl.Rev*. May 6, 2006, http://hir.harvard.edu/print/international-law/tuvalu-little-tuvalu-late

118 Revkin, Andrew. "Arctic Melt Unnerves the Experts." *NYTimes*. October 2, 2007, http://www.nytimes.com/2007/10/02/science/earth/02arct.html

119 "Global Warming." *NYTimes*. Updated September 30, 2011, http://topics.nytimes.com/top/news/science/topics/globalwarming/index.html#

120 Thompson, Lonnie. "Snows of Kilimanjaro Disappearing, Glacial Ice Loss Increasing." *ResearchNews*. Accessed October 29, 2011, http://researchnews.osu.edu/archive/scndkili.htm

121 "Conservation on Kilimanjaro." *ABCP*. last revised August 7, 2008, http://www.blackwoodconservation.org/kilimanjaro_conservation.html

122 "Raising Voices: The Kilimanjaro Native Co-operative Union." *Oxfam*. Accessed November 15, 2011, http://www.oxfam.org/en/campaigns/climatechange/kilimanjaro-native-co-operative-union

123 Revkin, Andrew. "Climate Debate Gets Its Icon: Mt. Kilimanjaro." *NYTimes*. March, 23, 2004, http://www.nytimes.com/2004/03/23/science/climate-debate-gets-its-icon-mt-kilimanjaro.html

124 "Forest Fires, Illegal Logging Threaten Mt. Kilimanjaro: Survey." *China View*. January 1, 2005, http://news.xinhuanet.com/english/2005-01/11/content_2445451.htm

125 "The Five Zones of Mt. Kilimanjaro." 4th Summit. Accessed November 15, 2011, http://www.4thsummit.com/mount-kili-manjaro-zones.aspx

126 Schmid, Randolph. "Mount Kilimanjaro Snow Cap Is Disappearing." *HuffPost*. November 2, 2011, http://www.huffingtonpost.com/2009/11/02/mount-kilimanjaro-snow-ca_n_342777.html

127 Glick, Daniel. "Signs From Earth: The Big Thaw." *NationalGeographic*. September 2004, accessed November 28, 2011, http://environment.nationalgeographic.com/environment/global-warming/big-thaw/#page=6

128 "National Party Identification (Registered and Likely Voters Only)." *HuffPost*. Updated October 10, 2010, http://www.huffingtonpost.com/2009/06/23/party-id-rl_n_725932.html

129 "Persons Reported Registered and Voted by State:1010." *Census.gov*. Accessed November 26, 2011, http://www.census.gov/compendia/statab/2012/tables/12s0400.pdf

130 "Leadership PACs." *Open secrets*. Accessed October 29, 2011, http://www.opensecrets.org/pacs/industry.php?txt=q03&cycle=2010

131 "Revolving Door: Former Members of the 111th Congress." *Open Secrets*. Accessed October 29, 2011, http://209.190.229.100/revolving/departing.php?cong=111

132 Forner, Eric. "'A New Birth of Freedom': Securing Emancipation." *The Fiery Trail: Abraham Lincoln and American Slavery* (New York: W.W. Norton, 2011) 266

133 Thomas, Bill, Hennessey, Keith, Holtz-Eakin, Douglas. "What Caused the Financial Crisis?" *WSJ*. January 27, 2011, http://online.wsj.com/article/SB10001424052748704698004576104500524998280.html

134 "Under the Influence: Special Interest Money and Members of Congress." *Clean Up Washington*. Accessed November 15, 2011, http://www.cleanupwashington.org/sii/

135 Kane, Paul. "Key Lawmakers in Health-Care Debate Reveal Investments in Health Industry." *Washington Post*. June 13,

2009, http://www.washingtonpost.com/wp-dyn/content/article/2009/06/12/AR2009061204075.html

136 Kroft, Steve. "Congress: Trading Stock on Inside Information?" *CBSNews.* November 13, 2011, http://www.cbsnews.com/8301-18560_162-57323527/congress-trading-stock-on-inside-information/

137 Froomkin, Dan. "Congress Increasingly Staffed By Former Lobbyists." *HuffPost.* July 12, 2011, http://www.huffington-post.com/2011/07/12/congress-increasingly-staffed-by-lobbyists_n_896389.html

138 Snow, Nancy. "Media, Terrorism, and the Politics of Fear." *WACC.* Accessed October 29, 2011, http://www. waccglobal.org/en/20073-media-and-terror/465-Media-terrorism-and-the-politics-of-fear.html

139 Balz, Dan. "Republicans: From 'Party of No' to 'Party of Stop'." *WashingtonPost.* September 23, 2010, http://www.washingtonpost.com/wp-dyn/content/article/2010/09/23/AR2010092302709.html

140 "Voters Reject Extreme Politics in Several Elections." *Bradenton.* November 12, 2011, http://www.bradenton.com/2011/11/12/3645690/miami-herald-editorial-voters.html

141 Goldberg, Jonah. "Too Uninformed to Vote?" *LATimes.* July 31, 2007, http://www.latimes.com/news/opinion/commentary/la-oe-goldberg31jul31,0,6430906.column

142 Caastillo, Cathy, Chang, Helen. "Why Your Smart Phone Makes You Dumb." *Stanford.edu.* March 23, 2011, http://www.stanford.edu/group/knowledgebase/cgi-bin/2011/03/23/why-your-smart-phone-makes-you-dumb/

143 Heierbacher, Sandy. "America Speaks Launches the American Square." *NCDD.* April 28, 2011, http://ncdd.org/5023

144 Sargent, Greg. "CNN Poll: Republicans Want Obama's Policies to Fail." *WashingtonPost.* October 18, 2011, http://www.washingtonpost.com/blogs/plum-line/post/cnn-poll-republicans-want-obamas-policies-to-fail/2011/10/18/gIQA-L0VbuL_blog.html

145 Cordes, Nancy. "Do Corporate Interests Rule Washington?" *CBSNews*. June 28, 2011, http://www.cbsnews.com/stories/2011/06/28/eveningnews/main20075218.shtml

146 "Forever Porous? *VVDailyPress*. November 14, 2011," http://www.vvdailypress.com/opinion/security-31290-border-patrol.html

147 Thee-Brenan, Megan, Elder, Janet. "Voters' Mood–Men Are Fuming, Women Despairing." *NYTimes*. September 21, 2010, http://www.nytimes.com/2010/09/21/us/politics/21poll.html

148 "Congressional Performance." *RasmussenReport*. October 24, 2011, http://www.rasmussenreports.com/public_content/politics/mood_of_america/congressional_performance

149 Proverbs 18:2.

150 Matthew 12:36-37.

151 James 1:26.

152 Proverbs 17:28.

153 James 1:22-25.

154 Proverbs 30:5–6.

155 "Northern Opposition to Lincoln." *HarpWeek*. Accessed October 29, 2011, http://elections.harpweek.com/1864/overview-1864-1.htm#Opposition

156 Reich, Robert. "Rick Perry's Secret Plan to Save Blue States From Red States." *HuffPost*. August 31, 2011, http://www.huffingtonpost.com/robert-reich/post_2351_b_943232.html

157 Blake, Aaron, Weiner, Rachel. "Blue Dog Democrats a Dying Breed." *WashingtonPost*. July 26, 2011, http://www.washingtonpost.com/blogs/the-fix/post/blue-dog-democrats-a-dying-breed/2011/07/25/gIQA7KGoaI_blog.html

158 "Insurance." *OpenSecret*. October 31, 20011, http://www.opensecrets.org/industries/indus.php?ind=F09

159 Buetler, Brian. "House Dems Press GOP to Abandon Their Federal Health Benefits." November 18, 1010, http://tpmdc.talkingpointsmemo.com/2010/11/house-dems-press-gop-to-abandon-their-federal-health-benefits.php

160 Levey, Naom. "U.S. Healthcare Spending Far Outpaces Other Countries." *LATimes*. June 30, 2011, http://articles.latimes.com/2011/jun/30/news/la-heb-health-spending-20110630

161 Murray, M.D., Christopher, Frenk, M.D., Julio. "Ranking 37th–Measuring the Performance of U.S. Health Care System." *NEJM*. January 14, 2010, http://www.nejm.org/doi/full/10.1056/NEJMp0910064

162 "U.S. Ranks Just 42nd in Life Expectancy." *MSNBC*. Updated August 11, 2007, http://www.msnbc.msn.com/id/20228552/ns/health-health_care/t/us-ranks-just-nd-life-expectancy/

163 Barry-Jester, Anna Maria. "U.S. Newborn Mortality Rate Higher Than In 40 Countries." *ABCNews*. September 1, 2011, http://abcnews.go.com/MillionMomsChallenge/us-newborn-mortality-rate-higher-40-countries/story?id=14420009

164 "The Price of Excess: Identifying waste in Healthcare Spending." *PCW*. Accessed November 16, 2011, http://www.pwc.com/us/en/healthcare/publications/the-price-of-excess.jhtml

165 Aizenman, N.C. "New Study Shows Health Insurance Premium Spikes in Every State." *WashingtonPost*. November 17, 2011, http://www.washingtonpost.com/national/health-science/new-study-shows-health-insurance-premium-spikes-in-every-state/2011/11/16/gIQAhBl7SN_story.html

166 "What Is Single Payer?" *PNHP*. January 11, 2010, http://www.pnhp.org/print/facts/what-is-single-payer

167 Heady, M.D., Bernadine. "Electronic Medical Records: Will Your Privacy Be Safe?" *USNews*. February 17, 2009, http://health.usnews.com/health-news/blogs/heart-to-heart/2009/02/17/electronic-medical-records-will-your-privacy-be-safe

168 Santiago, Andrea. "What Is Tort Reform?" *About.com*. Accessed November 18, 2011, http://healthcareers.about.com/od/healthcareerissues/f/TortReform.htm

169 "Wall Street and the Financial Crisis: Anatomy of Financial Collapse." *HSGAC*. Accessed November 1, 2011, http://

hsgac.senate.gov/public/_files/Financial_Crisis/Financial-CrisisReport.pdf

170 Woellert, Lorraine. "DeMarco Defends Executive Pay at Fannie Mae and Freddie Mac." *Bloomberg*. November 10, 2011, http://www.bloomberg.com/news/2011-11-10/fannie-mae-freddie-mac-executive-pay-defended-by-chief-regulator-demarco.html

171 Myerson, Harold. "China's Bad Economic News Is Not Necessarily Good News for the U.S." *WashingtonPost*. May 10, 2011, http://www.washingtonpost.com/opinions/chinas-bad-economic-news-is-not-necessarily-good-for-the-us/2011/05/10/AFaxZ3jG_story.html

172 "Government Urged Not to Ease Restrictions on U.S. Beef Imports." *JapanPress*. April 7–13, 2010, http://www.japan-press.co.jp/modules/news/index.php?id=285

173 Liu, John. "Yuan Drops Most in Four Months On Signs China Is Halting Gains." Bloomberg. May 26. 2009, http://www.bloomberg.com/apps/news?pid=newsarchive&sid=alrpw0Y4k9.o&refer=home

174 Spruiell, Stephen. "Protectionism – Tariffs, Subsidies, and Trade Policy." *GlobalEnvision*. August 30, 2006, http://www.globalenvision.org/library/15/1211

175 Johnson, Alex. "Bush Signs $700 Billion Financial Bailout Bill." *MSNBC*. October 3, 2008, http://www.msnbc.msn.com/id/26987291/ns/business-stocks_and_economy/t/bush-signs-billion-financial-bailout-bill/#

176 "How Rumsfeld Abandoned the Peacemakers." *DailyBeast/NewsWeek*. February 6, 2011, http://www.thedailybeast.com/newsweek/2011/02/06/how-rumsfeld-abandoned-the-peacemakers.html

177 Wike, Richard. "From Hyperpower to Declining Power." *PewResearchCenter*. September 7, 2011, http://pew-global.org/2011/09/07/from-hyperpower-to-declining-power/?src=prc-headline

178 Zoroya, Gregg. "Troops' Families Feel Weight of War." *USAToday*. August 4, 2009, http://www.usatoday.com/news/military/2009-08-03-broken-families_N.htm

179 Blankley, Tony. "Blankley: Bring Back the Draft." *Washington-Times*. February 11, 2009," http://www.washingtontimes.com/news/2009/feb/11/bring-back-the-draft/print/

180 "Is the U.S. Army Losing Its War on Suicide?" *Time*. April 13, 2010, http://www.time.com/time/printout/0,8816,1981284,00.html#

181 "1 in 8 Returning Soldiers Suffers From PTSD." *MSNBC*. Updated June 30, 2009, http://www.msnbc.msn.com/id/5334479/ns/health-mental_health/t/returning-soldiers-suffers-ptsd/

182 "Mental Health Effects of Serving in Iraq and Afghanistan." *PTSD.VA*. Created January 1, 2007, http://www.ptsd.va.gov/public/pages/overview-mental-health-effects.asp

183 Herbert, Bob. "The Lunatic Manual." *NYTimes*. August 2, 2010, http://www.nytimes.com/2010/08/03/opinion/03herbert.html

184 Hanson, Gordon. "The Economic Logic of Illegal Immigration." *CouncilOnForeignRealtions*. Updated March 15, 2007, accessed November 16, 2011, http://www.cfr.org/immigration/economic-logic-illegal-immigration/p12969

185 Gavett, Gretchen. "Record Number of Illegal Immigrants Deported in 2011." *PBS*. October 18, 2011, http://www.pbs.org/wgbh/pages/frontline/race-multicultural/lost-in-detention/record-number-of-illegal-immigrants-deported-in-2011/

186 Number of Illegal Immigrants Plunges by 1M." CBSNews. February 11, 2010, http://www.cbsnews.com/stories/2010/02/11/national/main6197466.shtml

187 Gavett, Gretchen. "Study: 5,100 Kids in Foster Care After Parents Deported." *PBS*. November 3, 2011, http://www.pbs.org/wgbh/pages/frontline/race-multicultural/lost-in-detention/study-5100-kids-in-foster-care-after-parents-deported/

188 Elk, Mike. "Undocumented Workers Paid $11.4 Billion in Taxes while GE Paid Nothing." *Think Progress*. April 23, 2011 at

10:23, http://thinkprogress.org/security/2011/04/23/176576/immigrants-taxes-general-electric

189 Unnikrishnan, Kesavan. "Chinese iPad Factory Workers Forced to Sign No-Suicide Pacts." *Digital Journal*. May 8, 2011, http://digitaljournal.com/print/article/306462

190 Velasquez, M., Andre, C., Shanks, T., Meyer M.J. "*Common-Good*." accessed November 2, 2011, http://www.scu.edu/ethics/practicing/decision/commongood.html

191 Healy, Melissa. "Tough Love for Fat People: Tax Their Food to Pay for Healthcare." *LATimes*. July 27,2009, http://latimes-blogs.latimes.com/booster_shots/2009/07/tough-love-for-fatties-tax-their-food-pay-for-healthcare.html

192 Snyder, Myles. "Teen Rescued After 'Thrill Seeking' Jump Into Susquehanna." *ABC27*. Updated October 17, 2011, http://www.abc27.com/story/15711532/teen-rescued-after-thrill-seeking-jump-into-susquehanna

193 Knoy, Laura. "Individual Rights and the Common Good." *NHPR*. October 19, 2009, http://www.nhpr.org/node/27280

194 Patsuris, Penelope. "The Corporate Scandal Sheet." *Forbes*. Aug. 26, 2002, http://www.forbes.com/2002/07/25/accoun-tingtracker.html

195 Cooper, Michael. "Deep Recession Sharply Altered U.S. Jobless Map." *NYTimes*. September 26, 2011, http://www.nytimes.com/2011/09/27/us/unrelenting-downturn-is-redrawing-americas-economic-map.html?pagewanted=all

196 Gomstyn, Alice. "Bailout Bill Basics: From TARP to Tax Breaks." *ABC News*. Oct. 2, 2008. http://abcnews.go.com/Business/Economy/story?id=5932586&page=1

197 Weston, Liz. "Lenders Create a Bankruptcy Monster." *MoneyCentralMSN*. Accessed November 17, 2010, http://articles.moneycentral.msn.com/Banking/BankruptcyGuide/LendersCreateABankruptcyMonster.aspx

198 Judson,Bruce."RestoringCapitalism:UnequalJustice—Banker Arrests 0; Protester Arrests 2,511." *HuffPost*. October 27, 2011, http://www.huffingtonpost.com/bruce-judson/occupy-arrests_b_1034907.html

199 Kelly, Ronald. "We're Mortgaging Our Children's Future." *UCG*. January 7, 2011, http://www.ucg.org/commentary/were-mortgaging-our-childrens-future/

200 Ollman, Bertell. "Market Economies: Advantages and Disadvantages." *NYU*. October 1999, accessed November 2, 2011, http://www.nyu.edu/projects/ollman/docs/china_speech2.php

201 Admin. "Report: 1,300 Children Killed in Mexico's Drug War." *LincolnTribune*. July 13, 2011, http://lincolntribune.com/?p=16175

202 "Mexico Under Siege: The Drug War At Our Doorstep." *LATimes*. November 16, 2011, http://projects.latimes.com/mexico-drug-war/#/its-a-war

203 Gannon, Kathy. "Taliban Gains Money, Al-Qaeda Finances Recovering." *CBSNews*. June 22, 2009, http://www.cnsnews.com/node/49886

204 Donadio, Rachel. "New Course for Antidrug Efforts in Afghanistan." *NYTimes*. June 27, 2009, http://www.nytimes.com/2009/06/28/world/asia/28holbrooke.html

205 Seidman, Andrew. "Senators Press Officials on Afghan Drug Trafficking." *NYTimes*. July 20, 2011, http://www.nytimes.com/2009/06/28/world/asia/28holbrooke.html

206 Suddath, Claire. "Brief History of War on Drugs." *Time*. March 25, 2009, http://www.time.com/time/world/ article/0,8599,1887488,00.html

207 Carter, Jimmy. "Call Off the Global Drug War." *NYTimes*. June 16, 2011, http://www.nytimes.com/2011/06/17/opinion/17carter.html

208 "Secretary Napolitano Announces Fiscal Year 2012 Budget Request." *DHS*. February 14, 2011, http://www.dhs.gov/ynews/releases/pr_1297696999494.shtm

209 Lasica, J. D. "What Is Participatory Journalism?" *OJR*. August 7, 2003, http://www.ojr.org/ojr/workplace/1060217106.php

210 Farhi, Douglas. "Political Pundits, Overpopulating the News Networks." *WashingtonPost*. February 19, 2008, http://

www.washingtonpost.com/wp-dyn/content/article/2008/02/18/AR2008021802267.html

211 Mirkinson, Jack. "Cable News Ratings: Top 30 Ratings Programs in Q2 2010 (Photos)." *HuffPost*. June 30, 2010, http://www.huffingtonpost.com/2010/06/30/cable-news-ratings-top-30_n_630984.html#s108333&title=1_The_OReilly

212 Sullivan, Meg. "Media Bias Is Real, Finds UCLA Political Scientist." *NewsRoom.UCLA*. December 14, 2005, *UCLA*. http://newsroom.ucla.edu/portal/ucla/Media-Bias-Is-Real-Finds-UCLA-6664.aspx

213 "Voter Anger Tilts Balance of Power in Congress Again." *SunSentinel*. November 3, 2010, http://articles.sun-sentinel.com/2010-11-03/news/fl-2010-elections-congress-editorial-20101103_1_tea-party-movement-balanced-budget-voter

214 "Minority Babies Set to Become the Majority in 2010." *MSNBC*. Updated March 10, 20110, http://www.msnbc.msn.com/id/35793316/ns/us_news-life/t/minority-babies-set-become-majority/

215 Cohen, Adam. "Supreme Court Ruling on Corporate Donations." *Time*. July 7, 2011, http://www.time.com/time/nation/article/0,8599,2001844,00.html

216 "Bush v. Gore." *4LawSchool*. Accessed November 2, 2011, http://www.4lawschool.com/conlaw/bg.shtml

217 "The Judicial Branch: U.S. Constitution, art. III, sec. 1, 2, & 3" *USConstitution*. Accessed November 17, 2011, http://www.usconstitution.net/const.html#Article3

218 Taranto, James. "What Is 'Judicial Activism'?" *WSJ*. February 9, 2011, http://online.wsj.com/article/SB1000142405274870485840457613427311321194 8.html

219 Kochhar, R., Fry, R., Taylor, P. "Wealth Gaps Rise to Record Levels Between Whites, Blacks and Hispanics." *Pew Research Center*. July 26, 2011, http://pewresearch.org/pubs/2069/housing-bubble-subprime-mortgages-hispanics-blacks-household-wealth-disparity

220 Ransel, Vi. "The Plight of Mass Unemployment in America. What Are the Causes?" *GlobalResearch.CA*. March 29, 2010. http://www.globalresearch.ca/index.php?context=va&aid=18393

221 Pace, Julie. "Obama: End Tax Breaks That Send Jobs Overseas." *CBSNews*. October 10, 2010, http://www.cbsnews.com/stories/2010/10/16/politics/main6964121.shtml

222 Ross, Janell. "Major American Brands Silent on Alleged Rights Abuses At Overseas Factories." *HuffPost*. July 21, 2011, http://www.huffingtonpost.com/2011/07/21/american-brands-abuses-factories-jordan-labor-conditions_n_903995.html?view=screen

223 Hatch, David. "High Tech, Low Standards." *NationalJournal*. April 28, 2011, http://www.nationaljournal.com/magazine/high-tech-low-standards-20110428

224 Burke, Heather. "Mattel Recall of Chinese Toys Will Cost $30 Million (Update5)" *Bloomberg*. August 2, 2007, http://www.bloomberg.com/apps/news?pid=newsarchive&sid=ayKvA4ZBQ45Q

225 Schneider, Andrew. "Imported Seafood May Be Riskier Than Gulf Fare." *AOL*. August 25, 2010, http://www.aolnews.com/2010/08/26/worried-about-gulf-   seafood-imports-may-be-bigger-risk/

226 Burns, Robert. "Activities in China That May Constitute U.S. Patent Infringement." *ChinaIPNews*. June 2008, http://www.finnegan.com/resources/articles/articlesdetail.aspx?news=bb6566c1-5fd8-476e-a13a-4f301c4244e4

227 "Country-of-Origin Labeling." *ERS.USDA*. Updated October 2, 2007, http://www.ers.usda.gov/features/cool/

228 Hsu, Tiffany. "Trade Deficit With China Cost Nearly 2.8 Million U.S. Jobs Since 2001." *LATimes*. September 22, 2011, http://latimesblogs.latimes.com/money_co/2011/09/trade-deficit-with-china-cost-nearly-28-million-us-jobs-since-2001.html

229 "Government Urged Not to Ease Restrictions on U.S. Beef Imports." *JapanPress*. April 7–13, 2010, http://www.japan-press.co.jp/modules/news/index.php?id=285

230 "Wis. Governor Officially Cuts Collective Bargaining." *MSNBC*. March 11, 2011, http://www.msnbc.msn.com/id/41996994/ns/politics-more_politics/t/wis-governor-officially-cuts-collective-bargaining/

231 Seegal, Hallie. "Eight Surprising Facts about the Shrinking Middle Class." *HuffPost*. August 9, 2010, http://www.huffingtonpost.com/2010/08/09/8-surprising-facts-about_n_675545.html#s121657&title=Income_Inequality_Is

232 Celock, John. "Ohio SB 5 Collective Bargaining Law Follows Efforts in Wisconsin and New Jersey." *HuffPost*. September 21, 2011, http://www.huffingtonpost.com/2011/09/20/ohio-sb5-referendum-collective-bargaining_n_972321.html

233 Berman, Jullian. "Tax Cuts For Wealthy Americans Costs Treasury $11.6 Million Every Hour: Report" *HuffPost*. November 18, 2011, http://www.huffingtonpost.com/2011/10/14/tax-cuts-for-wealthy-americans_n_1011601.html

234 Aversa, Jeannine. "Treasury Secretary: Social Security Has No 'Real' Assets." *Google*. *EllensburgDailyTimes*. July 18, 2001, accessed November 18, 2011, http://news.google.com/newspapers?nid=860&dat=20010718&id=MTEfAAAAIBAJ&sjid=IccEAAAAIBAJ&pg=5186,1962846

235 Gold, Howard. "Kiss the AAA Rating of the U.S. Goodbye." *MarketWatch*. July 27, 2011, http://www.marketwatch.com/story/kiss-the-aaa-rating-of-the-us-goodbye-2011-07-27

236 Montopoli, Brian, Jackson, Jill. "Pledge to America' Unveiled by Republicans." *CBSNews*. September 22, 2010, http://www.cbsnews.com/8301-503544_162-20017335-503544.html

237 Proverbs 6:10–11

238 Ellis, Blake. "Delaying Retirement: 80 is the New 65." *Money*. *CNN*. November 16, 2011, http://money.cnn.com/2011/11/16/retirement/age/index.htm

239 Mittleberger, Gottlieb. "Gottlieb Mittleberger on Indentured Servitude." *Faulkner.edu*. Accessed November 3, 2011, http://www.faulkner.edu/academics/artsandsciences/socialandbehavioral/readings/hy/servitude.aspx

240 Morris, Richard B. "The Emergence of American Labor." *United States Department of Labor.* http://www.dol.gov/oasam/programs/history/chapter1.htm

241 "The Cotton Economy of the Old South." *IAState.* Accessed November 3, 2011, http://www.history.iastate.edu/agprimer/Page28.html

242 Janiskee, Bob. "Sullivan Island Was the African-American Ellis Island." *National Parks Traveler.* http://www.nationalparkstraveler.com/2009/03/sullivan-s-island-african-american-ellis-island

243 Greenhouse, Steven. "Strained States Turn to Laws to Curb Labor Unions." *New York Times.* January 3, 2011, http://www.nytimes.com/2011/01/04/business/04labor.html?pagewanted=all

244 "Corporate Myths About Shipping Jobs Overseas." *AFLCIO.* Accessed November 28, 2011, http://www.aflcio.org/issues/jobseconomy/jobs/outsourcing_myths.cfm

245 Secunda, Paul. "NLRB Complains About Boeing's Move to South Carolina." *SeattleTimes.* April 29, 2011, http://seattletimes.nwsource.com/html/northwestvoices/2014910359_nlrbcomplainsaboutboeingsmovetosouthcarolina.html

246 Ford, Andréa. "A Brief History of NAFTA." *Time.* December 30, 2008, http://www.time.com/time/nation/article/0,8599,1868997,00.html

247 Parks, James. "The Future of Manufacturing and America's Middle Class." *AFL-CIO.* Accessed November 3, 2011, http://www.aflcio.org/aboutus/thisistheaflcio/publications/magazine/0404_manufacturing.cfm

248 Sawyer, Diane. "'Made in America' Pledge: What is American-Made in Your Home?" *ABCNews.* Accessed November 17, 2011, http://abcnews.go.com/WN/MadeInAmerica/mailform?id=12912252

249 McWorld Staff. "Inside Apple's iPod Factories." *McWorld.* June 12, 2006, http://www.macworld.co.uk/mac/news/?newsid=14915

250 Jingjing, Jiang. "Wal-Mart's China Inventory to Hit US$18b This Year." *ChinaDaily*. Updated November 29, 2004, accessed November 18, 2011, http://www.chinadaily.com.cn/english/doc/2004-11/29/content_395728.htm

251 Ross, Lee, Associate Press. "Supreme Court Removes Limits on Corporate, Labor Donations to Campaigns." *FoxNews*. January 21, 2010, http://www.foxnews.com/politics/2010/01/21/supreme-court-sides-hillary-movie-filmmakers-campaign-money-dispute/

252 "Mitt Romney Says 'Corporations Are People' at Iowa State Fair." *Washington Post*. August 28, 2011, http://www.washingtonpost.com/politics/mitt-romney-says-corporations-are-people/2011/08/11/gIQABwZ38I_story.html

253 Daly, Corbett. "Obama Says He Cannot Guarantee Social Security Checks Will Go Out." *CBSNews*. July 12, 2011, http://www.cbsnews.com/8301-503544_162-20078789-503544.html

254 Matthews, Merrill. "What Happened to $2.6 Trillion Social Security Trust Fund?" *Forbes*. July 13, 2011, http://blogs.forbes.com/merrillmatthews/2011/07/13/what-happened-to-the-2-6-trillion-social-security-trust-fund/

255 Wetzel, Kara, Maurus, Christine. "U.S. Homes 'Underwater" on Loans Drop as Foreclosures Mount." *Businessweek*. December 13, 2010, http://news.businessweek.com/article.asp?documentKey=1376-LRFIR76K50XS01-4KO5M66PBE5R-GA0I7UMRPTF2A5

256 Lee, Amy. "Apple Manufacturer Foxconn Makes Employees Sign 'No Suicide' Pact." *HuffPost*. Updated July 6, 2011, http://www.huffingtonpost.com/2011/05/06/apple-foxconn-suicide-pact_n_858504.html

257 "Study: More Think News Stories Are Biased." *MSNBC*. September 14, 2009, http://www.msnbc.msn.com/id/32832992/ns/us_news-life/t/study-more-think-news-stories-are-biased/

258 "Says Mitt Romney's Housing Policy is 'Don't Try and Stop the Foreclosure Process. Let It Run Its Course and Hit Bottom.'" *Politifact*. Accessed November 21, 2011, http://www.

politifact.com/truth-o-meter/statements/2011/nov/01/
democratic-national-committee/ad-claims-mitt-romneys-
housing-policy-let-foreclos/

259 "Occupy Wall Street." *HuffPost*. Accessed November 28, 2011, http://www.huffingtonpost.com/news/occupy-wall-street

260 "Arab Spring: Timeline of the African and Middle East Rebellions. *TheTelegraph*. October 21, 2011, http://www.telegraph.co.uk/news/worldnews/africaandindianocean/libya/8839143/Arab-Spring-timeline-of-the-African-and-Middle-East-rebellions.html

261 Strachan, Maxwell. "Corporate Tax Revenues Nearing Historic Lows As a Percentage of GDP, Report Says." *HuffPost*. March 2, 2011, http://www.huffingtonpost.com/2011/03/02/corporate-tax-revenues-ne_n_830361.html

262 Blake, Rich, Fahmy, Dalia. "Hoarding Not Hiring: Corporations Stockpiling Mountain of Cash." *ABCNews*. April 1, 2010, http://abcnews.go.com/Business/hoarding-hiring-corporations-stockpile-mountain-cash/story?id=10250559

263 Kocieniewski, David. "G.E.'s Strategies Let It Avoid Taxes Altogether." *NYTimes*. March 24, 2011, http://www.nytimes.com/2011/03/25/business/economy/25tax.html?pagewanted=all

264 "A Look At the World's New Corporate Tax Havens." *CBSNews*. March 25, 2011, http://www.cbsnews.com/stories/2011/03/25/60minutes/main20046867.shtml

265 "Employment Situation Summary." *BLS.gov*. November 4, 2011, http://www.bls.gov/news.release/empsit.nr0.htm

266 Harris, Paul. The Decline and Fall of the American Middle Class." *The Guardian*. September 13, 2011, http://www.guardian.co.uk/commentisfree/cifamerica/2011/sep/13/american-middle-class-poverty

267 Tavarnise, Sabrina. "Soaring Poverty Casts Spotlight on 'Lost Decade'".*NYTimes*.September 13, 2011, http://www.nytimes.com/2011/09/14/us/14census.html?pagewanted=all

268 Geewax, Marilyn. "More Americans Hungry For Food Stamps." *NPR*. August 28, 2011, http://www.npr.org/2011/08/28/

139968385/slow-growth-economy-spikes-food-stamp-reliance

269 Shapiro, Ari. "The Man Behind The GOP's No-Tax Pledge." NPR. July 14, 2011, http://www.npr.org/2011/07/14/137800715/the-man-behind-the-gops-tax-pledge

270 "Countries: China." EuropeanCommission. Accessed November 21, 2011, http://ec.europa.eu/trade/creating-opportunities/bilateral-relations/countries/china/

271 Kennedy, Simon, Adam, Shamim. "G-20 to Avoid 'Competitive Devaluation,' Prod China." Bloomberg. October 25, 2010, http://www.bloomberg.com/news/2010-10-24/g-20-vows-to-avoid-weakening-currencies-as-leaders-prepare-to-prod-china.html

272 "The Chinese in Africa." TheEconomist. April 20, 2011, http://www.economist.com/node/18586448

273 "China Became Largest Trading Partner of ASEAN." ChinaTimes. August 2011, accessed November 22, 2011, http://www.thechinatimes.com/online/2011/08/1025.html

274 Forero, Juan. "China and Brazil Warm Up Business, Culture Ties." NPR. June 29, 2011, http://www.npr.org/2011/06/29/137353744/china-and-brazil-warm-up-business-culture-ties

275 "China Surpasses U.S. as EU's Top Trade Partner: MOC" Xinhuanet.com. October 16, 2011, http://news.xinhuanet.com/english2010/china/2011-10/16/c_131194386.htm

276 Hounshell, Blake. "China Is Now Iran's Top Trading Partner." ForeignPolicy.com. February 9, 2010, http://blog.foreignpolicy.com/posts/2010/02/09/china_is_now_irans_top_trading_partner

277 Blustein, Paul. "China Passes U.S. In Trade With Japan." WashingtonPost. January 27, 2005, http://www.washington-post.com/wp-dyn/articles/A40192-2005Jan26.html

278 Andina. "China May Become Peru's Top Trade Partner by the End of 2011." PeruThisWeek. October 5, 2011, http://www.peruthisweek.com/news-748-China-may-become-Peru%C3%A2%E2%82%AC%E2%84%A2s-top-trade-partner-by-the-end-of-2011/

279 "China to Become Russia's Largest Trading Partner." *RussiaBriefing*. March 10, 2011, http://russia-briefing.com/news/china-to-become-russias-largest-trading-partner.html/

280 "China Holds More U.S. Debt Than Indicated." *Washington-Times*. March 2, 2010, http://www.washingtontimes.com/news/2010/mar/2/chinas-debt-to-us-treasury-more-than-indicated/?page=all

281 "U.S. Credit Rating Downgraded." *NPR*. August 6, 2011, http://www.npr.org/2011/08/06/139046367/u-s-credit-rating-downgraded

282 Taylor, Andrew. "Super Committee Failure Sets Up Partisan Wrangling In Congress." *HuffPost*. November 22, 2011, http://www.huffingtonpost.com/2011/11/22/super-committee-failure_n_1107845.html

283 "Utility in Pipeline Blast Still 'Looking Into' Odor Complaints." *MSNBC*. Updated September 10, 2010, http://www.msnbc.msn.com/id/39089768/ns/us_news/t/utility-pipeline-blast-still-looking-odor-complaints/

284 "9 Thought Dead As Minneapolis Bridge Collapses." *MSNBC*. August 2, 2007, http://www.msnbc.msn.com/id/20079534/ns/us_news-life/t/thought-dead-minneapolis-bridge-collapses/

285 "Shinkansen." *Japan Guide*. Accessed November 28, 2011, http://www.japan-guide.com/e/e2018.html

286 Hunt, Katrina Brown. "Best and Worst Airports for Delays." *TravelandLeisure*. November 2011, http://www.travelandleisure.com/articles/best-and-worst-airports-for-delays

287 Kastenbaum, Steve. "U.S. High-Speed Rail System Hit by Deep Budget Cuts." *CNN*. April 13, 2011,

288 "California Blackout A Reminder of U.S. Power Grid Vulnerability." *FoxNews*. September 10, 2011, http://www.foxnews.com/us/2011/09/10/california-blackout-reminder-us-power-grid-vulnerability/

289 Pelley, Scott. "Homeless Veterans: Trying To Find Help and Hope." *CBSNews*. October 14, 2010, http://www.cbsnews.com/stories/2010/10/14/60minutes/main6958101.shtml

290 Beucke, Dan. "Unemployment for Young Vets: 30%, and Rising." *BusinessWeek*. November 11, 2011, http://www.businessweek.com/finance/occupy-wall-street/archives/2011/11/the_vets_job_crisis_is_worse_than_you_think.html

291 Yeebo, Yepoka. "As CEO Pay Soars, Many New Jobs Fail to Provide a Living Wage." *HuffPost*. April 1, 2011, http://www.huffingtonpost.com/2011/04/01/ceo-pay-living-wage_n_843481.html

292 Nussbaum, Bruce. "The Truth Behind China's BYD Car Company—And Warren Buffet's Investment." *Businessweek*. Feb. 11, 2011, http://www.businessweek.com/innovate/NussbaumOnDesign/archives/2010/02/the_truth_behin.html

293 Martin, Ray. "Children's Allowance: What and When to Pay." *CBSNews*. June 30, 2010, http://www.cbsnews.com/8301-505146_162-39640411/childrens-allowance-what-and-when-to-pay/

294 Barabak, Mark. "Perry's Climate Views Shared By 'Tea Party' Faithful, Survey Says." *LATimes*. September 9, 2011, http://articles.latimes.com/2011/sep/09/news/la-pn-perry-climate-tea-party-20110909

295 Condon, Stephanie. "Will Republicans Abandon 'Drill, Baby, Drill'?" *CBSNews*. April 30, 2010, http://www.cbsnews.com/8301-503544_162-20003924-503544.html

296 "Regulating U.S. Into Economic Destruction." *Tea Party.org*. Accessed November 17, 2011, http://www.teaparty.org/article.php?id=1226

297 Zandi, Mark. "A Federal Shutdown Could Derail the Recovery." *Moody's Analytics*. February 21, 2011, http://www.economy.com/dismal/article_free.asp?cid=197630&src=wp

298 Frank, Robert. "In the Real World of Work and Wages, Trickle-Down Theories Don't Hold Up." *NYTimes*. April 12, 2007,

299 Smith, Charles. "Why the Fed's 'Trickle-Down Economics' is Failing." *DailyFinance*. October 25, 2010, http://www.dailyfinance.com/2010/10/25/why-the-feds-trickle-down-economics-is-failing/

300 Cohan, Peter. "Do Tax Cuts Create Jobs?" *Forbes*. May 3, 2011. http://blogs.forbes.com/petercohan/2011/05/03/do-tax-cuts-create-jobs/

301 "Governor Says Texans May Want to Secede from the Union but Probably Won't." *Fox News*. April 15, 2009, http://www.foxnews.com/politics/2009/04/15/governor-says-texans-want-secede-union-probably-wont/

302 Daly, Corbett. "FAA Left Hanging as Congress Leaves for August Recess." *CBSNews*. August 3, 2011, http://www.cbsnews.com/8301-503544_162-20087475-503544.html

303 "Melissa Brookstone, Tea Party Member, Suggests Small Businesses Stop Hiring to Oppose Obama." *HuffPost*. October 19, 2011, http://www.huffingtonpost.com/2011/10/19/tea-party-melissa-brookstone-occupy-wall-street_n_1020710.html

304 "Revenue Limits." *EdSource.org*. Accessed November 22, 2011, http://www.edsource.org/iss_fin_sys_revlimits.html

305 "State Rep. James White Proposes Revenue Neutral School Finance Reform." *TexasInsider*. February 28, 2011, http://www.texasinsider.org/?p=43196

306 "Is School Funding Fair? A National Report Card." *SchoolFundingFairness.org*. October 12, 2010. http://www.schoolfundingfairness.org/

307 McCartney, Kathleen. "Cutting Head Start Is Bad Fiscal Policy." *CNN*. March 14, 2011, http://edition.cnn.com/2011/OPINION/03/14/mccartney.head.start/index.html?hpt=Sbin

308 "Groups: Millions of U.S. Children Would Be Harmed by Proposed House Continuing Resolution Budget Cuts." *DigitalJournal*. March 9, 2011, http://www.digitaljournal.com/pr/242616

309 Armario, Christine. "'Wake-up Call': U.S. Students Trail Global Leaders." *MSNBC*. December 7, 2010, http://www.msnbc.msn.com/id/40544897/ns/us_news-life/t/wake-up-call-us-students-trail-global-leaders/

310 Weber, Joseph. "'Tea Party' Hopefuls Target Education Department." WashingtonTimes. October 25, 2010, http://

www.washingtontimes.com/news/2010/oct/25/tea-party-hopefuls-target-education-department/?page=all

311 "Should Your Child Have a Cell Phone?" *MySecureCyberspace*. Accessed November 22, 2011, http://www.mysecurecyber-space.com/articles/family-room/should-your-child-have-a-cell-phone.html

312 "Teachers Increasingly Value Media and Technology." *PBS. org*. Accessed November 22, 2011, http://www.pbs.org/teachers/_files/pdf/annual-pbs-survey-report.pdf

Index